the WHEEL of the YEAR

JESSICA ROUX

FIONA COOK

the WHEEL of the YEAR

An Illustrated Guide to Nature's Rhythms

Andrews McMeel
PUBLISHING®

For the readers & magic-makers who bring this book
to life, but especially, for Icarus & Orpheus.
—F.C.

For my mom, who always encouraged my love
of nature, reading, and the arts.
—J.R.

The Wheel of the Year

Andrews McMeel Publishing
a division of Andrews McMeel Universal
1130 Walnut Street, Kansas
City, Missouri 64106

www.andrewsmcmeel.com

23 24 25 26 27 RLP 10 9 8 7 6 5 4 3 2

ISBN: 978-1-5248-7480-3

Library of Congress
Control Number: 2023938124

Editor: Melissa Rhodes Zahorsky
Art Director/Designer: Diane Marsh
Production Editor: Dave Shaw
Production Manager: Tamara Haus

ATTENTION:
SCHOOLS AND BUSINESSES
Andrews McMeel books are available at
quantity discounts with bulk purchase
for educational, business, or sales
promotional use. For information,
please e-mail the Andrews McMeel
Publishing Special Sales Department:
sales@amuniversal.com.

Made by:
Shenzhen Reliance Printing Co., Ltd.
Address and place of manufacturer:
25 Longshan Industrial Zone, Nanling,
Longgang District,
Shenzhen, China, 518114
2nd Printing - 9/18/23

CONTENTS

LET'S BE SAFE!

Many of the activities in this book allow you to push your boundaries, have fun, build confidence, and learn new things. However, it's necessary to take care when trying something new. Life is all about finding that happy balance, after all.

GENERAL SAFETY

- Enter a mindset of care and concentration. Think of these activities as rituals: they work best if you take them seriously, giving them your full attention and respect.

- Read the activity through from start to finish before you begin. Gather all the tools and materials you'll need ahead of time.

- If an activity requires adult supervision, make sure your adult is aware of what's going on and is ready to be fully present.

- Listen respectfully if an adult gives feedback.

- Never be afraid to ask for help! Knowing your limits is a sign of power and maturity.

In the Kitchen

❖ Always have an adult around who can supervise or assist when you're using the stove, oven, or knives.

  Note: A few recipes in this book involve boiling water over the stove. It's especially important that an adult help with this. Just like fire, water is unpredictable!

❖ Use proper cooking tools: oven mitts or potholders, cutting boards, kitchen knives, etc.

❖ When using a knife, always cut away from yourself. If you've never used a sharp knife before, ask an adult to show you how. It may even be best to let them do the cutting.

❖ Wash your hands before touching ingredients. Keep all surfaces clean.

❖ If you have long hair, tie it back.

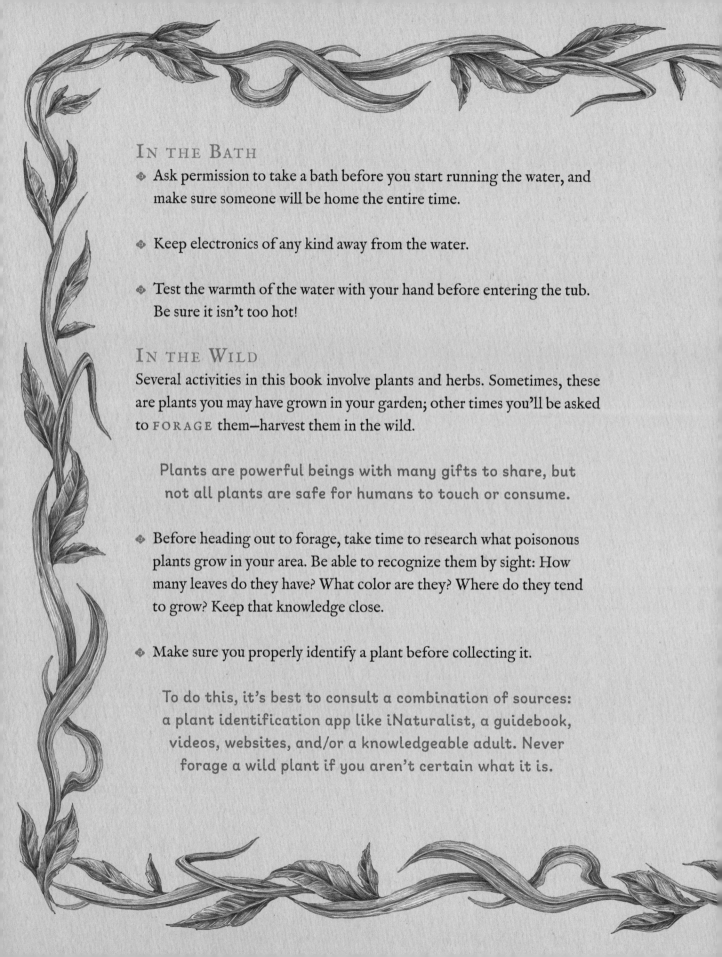

IN THE BATH

◆ Ask permission to take a bath before you start running the water, and make sure someone will be home the entire time.

◆ Keep electronics of any kind away from the water.

◆ Test the warmth of the water with your hand before entering the tub. Be sure it isn't too hot!

IN THE WILD

Several activities in this book involve plants and herbs. Sometimes, these are plants you may have grown in your garden; other times you'll be asked to FORAGE them—harvest them in the wild.

> Plants are powerful beings with many gifts to share, but not all plants are safe for humans to touch or consume.

◆ Before heading out to forage, take time to research what poisonous plants grow in your area. Be able to recognize them by sight: How many leaves do they have? What color are they? Where do they tend to grow? Keep that knowledge close.

◆ Make sure you properly identify a plant before collecting it.

> To do this, it's best to consult a combination of sources: a plant identification app like iNaturalist, a guidebook, videos, websites, and/or a knowledgeable adult. Never forage a wild plant if you aren't certain what it is.

- Wear a pair of gardening gloves to protect your hands while foraging. Long sleeves and pants can also be helpful. If touching a plant gives you a rash or makes your skin itchy, tell an adult right away.

- Take special care with berries! With their bright colors, berries can be tempting to taste, but you must be certain they are edible. If you determine they're safe to eat, wash them first so you don't get sick.

- Before using plants in a potion or recipe, rinse them thoroughly in the sink.

- While many plants have MEDICINAL or healing properties (see the Basic Herbarium on pages 62–64), they aren't a replacement for professional medical treatment. Any serious health condition or injury should be seen to by a doctor.

AROUND THE FIRE

- Whether you're lighting a candle or building a campfire, never make a fire without an adult present, and never leave one unattended. (See page 76 for more detailed fire safety tips.)

I t's all around you; it's inside of you.

This book is not so much about learning how to *do* magic. It is, first and foremost, about learning how to *find* and *recognize* magic.

Good news! Kids tend to be better at seeing it than grown-ups. Just because something can be explained by science doesn't mean it's not also magical.

Magic connects one living thing, such as yourself, to every other living thing. The universe is alive, and you are a part of it. As you build a relationship with your environment, you tap into the magic and power inside and beyond yourself.

The Earth and the Sun do a dance that turns the Wheel of the Year, orchestrating a symphony of change through its seasons. In this book, we follow the cycle of one year—the time it takes the Earth to make a single journey around the Sun.

The Wheel of the Year is divided into eight spokes: two Solstices, two Equinoxes, and four cross-quarter days that fall between those significant alignments between the Sun and the Earth. The Wheel of the Year is a PAGAN tool, used by people who follow a nature-based spiritual path. While these eight holidays fall on specific days of the year, the Wheel itself, like our planet, is always turning.

Follow the Wheel at your own pace, but try to acknowledge each holiday on or around its actual date. You don't have to throw a big, planned-in-advance party (though you certainly can!). The best way to celebrate is by doing something that has personal meaning and significance to *you*. You could stand before your altar (more about altars on page 16) giving thanks for specific things you're grateful for. Or you might set intentions (wishes, hopes, and prayers) for the coming six weeks between spokes. Go outside and spend time with your neighborhood, revisiting the same plants and trees around your home. Notice how they, and you, change throughout the course of a year. Take time to notice what makes each season—*each day!*—special.

WHEREVER YOU MAY LIVE, THERE'S A
RHYTHM TO THE SEASONS, AND FORMING
A RELATIONSHIP WITH YOUR HOME AND
ITS INHABITANTS IS TRUE MAGIC.

OSTARA:
Spring Equinox

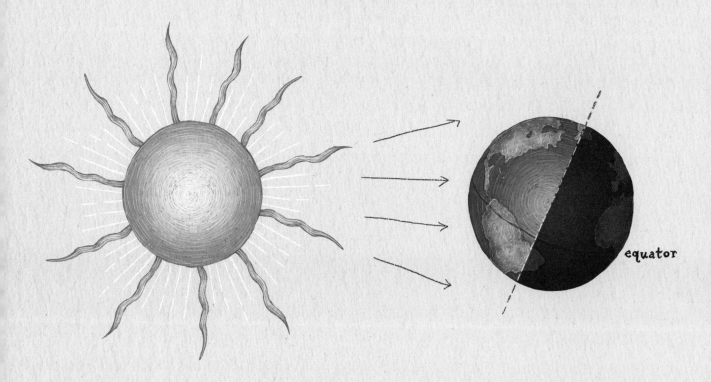

equator

RHYTHM OF THE WHEEL

Let's begin with Ostara—the Spring Equinox (also called the Vernal Equinox). Ostara is the dawn celebration of the Wheel of the Year. We emerge from the cold, dark days of Winter; leave behind what we no longer need; and take our first steps into new beginnings with purpose, lightness, and joy. It's a time of balance and renewal, with promises of longer days swirling in the air.

Equinox means *equal night:* there are exactly as many hours of daylight as there are of night, as the Sun shines directly onto the Earth's equator. This happens twice a year: on the first day of Spring and the first day of Autumn, and it happens because of the tilt of our Earth's axis.

If you're in the Northern Hemisphere, the days get a little longer following the Spring Equinox, but if you live in the Southern Hemisphere, the days will be shrinking.

SPIRIT OF THE SEASON

No matter where you live, you can celebrate the Spring Equinox. It's no coincidence that many of the themes of this holiday span place, time, and culture. A sense of possibility—of new beginnings—is in the very light and air.

Ostara is the season of buds, not blossoms. It's a yawn: a big, full-body stretch and a wiggling of the toes as the world warms up and gets ready to come alive. Ice is melting; the hard frozen ground begins to thaw. It's a time of softening and loosening. We made it through the darkest days of Winter. Now, we crack a window to clear out the stale air and let in the fresh breeze.

Some years, there might still be snow on the ground. But despite the unpredictable aspects of the season, there's always a tinge of hope. The temperature may be brisk, and we'll probably need a sweater and a hat on our walks outside, but we know that soon we'll be out in short sleeves.

Hope keeps us moving in the direction of light, life, and longer days. Take your time; you don't need to rush into anything. It's normal to sometimes feel a little overwhelmed by change, especially since we're still processing the lessons from Winter. If you feel hyper or pulled in too many directions, slow down. Focus on one thing: one small bud in a tree, or a single bird. The next six weeks until Beltane focus on growth, but also balance. Take them gradually, a little at a time, even if it's tempting to try to do everything at once.

KEEPING A JOURNAL

The words *journey* and *journal* come from the same root, meaning "one day." As you travel through a year, it's useful to notice patterns and keep track of progress.

A journal doesn't have to be anything fancy—in fact, sometimes a really nice blank book creates undue pressure to fill it with your Best Work. A journal isn't the place for best work! It's where you're allowed to be messy and uncertain. You don't have to worry what anyone else thinks, because it's for *you*. What you put in your journal doesn't have to look nice, or sound smart, funny, or cool.

You can jot down thoughts, sketch things you find beautiful or interesting, record your dreams, and keep track of magical occurrences. Sometimes, ideas float around only half-formed until you start putting them down on paper. You may surprise yourself with what shape your thoughts take as you write; it's a good way of getting to know yourself better. In your journal, you can be both speaker *and* listener.

Ideas for what to put in your journal:
❀ Self-portraits
❀ Poems
❀ Nature sketches
❀ Funny jokes
❀ Recipes
❀ Wishes
❀ Magazine cutouts
❀ Photos of people and things you like
❀ Tickets, invitations, or flyers from events that made you happy

How to use it:

You may find it useful to record a short sentence or two about what happened each day. Referring back later can help you identify patterns, cycles, and rhythms in the year.

It's good practice to keep track of SYNCHRONICITIES: uncanny coincidences (more on page 158). Most people have had some experience that defies normal explanation. Go ahead and ask the grown-ups you trust to be open with you: *Have you ever had something happen to you that you couldn't explain?* And find out what intriguing stories they have to share. The more you keep an eye out for peculiar, magical events, the more of them you'll find. File them away in your journal or share them with friends. You can even lend your journal to someone you trust and let them take over a page!

Many of the activities in this book—charcoal drawing (page 77), sigils (page 102), plant studies, homemade inks (page 99), just to name a few—can and should be recorded in your journal.

The more you use it, the more your journal will become like a physical extension of your self. So, what will you call your trusty friend? Here are a few ideas, though of course you should feel free to come up with your own name:

* Journey Around the Sun
* Journal of Waxing and Waning
* Book of Days
* Earth Book
* Synchronicities
* Pattern Book
* Rhythms of the Year
* Idea Journal
* Dreams and Imaginings

CELEBRATIONS: PAST & PRESENT

As far back as history goes, people have recognized the Spring Equinox. Ancient civilizations the world over built magnificent structures to showcase the stunning spectacle of the Equinox sunrise and sunset. It was, and remains, a time to rejoice in the natural balance of our universe. As the Wheel turns, people gather to witness the changes the new season promises, and to celebrate having made it through another harsh, barren Winter.

Unfortunately, throughout history some cultures' traditions have been lost as other people conquered and dominated them—especially if their traditions were passed along through storytelling and not written down. But many celebrations and rituals have survived and continue to be practiced to this day.

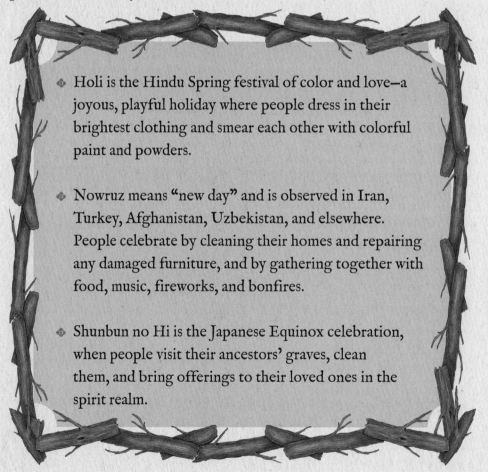

- Holi is the Hindu Spring festival of color and love—a joyous, playful holiday where people dress in their brightest clothing and smear each other with colorful paint and powders.

- Nowruz means "new day" and is observed in Iran, Turkey, Afghanistan, Uzbekistan, and elsewhere. People celebrate by cleaning their homes and repairing any damaged furniture, and by gathering together with food, music, fireworks, and bonfires.

- Shunbun no Hi is the Japanese Equinox celebration, when people visit their ancestors' graves, clean them, and bring offerings to their loved ones in the spirit realm.

STONEHENGE

Many stone circles, built as far back as 3000 BCE, remain around the British Isles and Ireland. Giant stones called MEGALITHS stand in fields, sometimes with other stones propped across them, called LINTELS. These

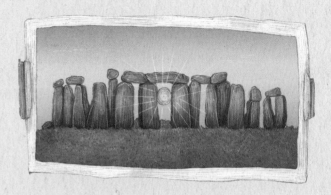

stone circles were likely gathering places for religious ceremonies, and served as ancient calendars, the Sun shining between them dramatically at the Solstices and Equinoxes. Stonehenge in modern-day Wiltshire, England, is the largest and most intact of the henges, and to this day, people gather to see the spectacle of light shining between its rocks.

CHICHEN ITZA

In the Yucatan region of Mexico, the ancient Mayan people built a stepped pyramid called the Temple of Kukulkan to honor their feathered serpent god. On the Equinoxes, the setting Sun brings to life an enormous snake of golden light that slithers down the side of the pyramid.

ANGKOR WAT

The largest religious monument in the world is the Buddhist temple complex Angkor Wat in Cambodia. Surrounded by a vast moat, the temple was designed to represent five-peaked Mount Meru, home of the gods and center of the physical and spiritual universes. Because of its east-west construction, the Sun rises directly over the center tower of the temple on the Equinox.

SCAVENGER HUNT

One of the best ways to celebrate the turning of the Wheel of the Year and its holidays is to go out and take a walk. It doesn't matter if you live in a city, the country, or somewhere in between, there will be changes from season to season. Look for small details; it's one of the best ways to show REVERENCE for our world. Some might call this observation a form of prayer.

We use our senses to gather information and gain an understanding of our surroundings. We're most familiar with the "big five"—sight, hearing, taste, touch, and smell—but that's a limited list. Plants and animals have senses, too, and not all the same ones we use.

SEE:
* A nest
* A catkin
* A bud on a tree
* A bulb poking out of the ground
* An earthworm

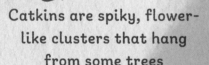

Catkins are spiky, flower-like clusters that hang from some trees

SMELL:
* Dirt
* Something rotting
* Rain

HEAR:
* A goose honking
* A baby bird calling out to be fed
* A seagull cawing
* A chickadee chirping
* The wind

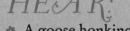

Plants, for instance, have senses for moisture and light. They stretch and grow toward dampness with their roots, and toward sunlight with their leaves. A dog's nose is so much more sensitive than ours that it can detect emotion, danger, and changes in the weather.

Not everyone has use of all five typical senses, but every living thing uses what tools it has to organize its perception of the world. Use what tools *you* have to see how many of these signs of Ostara you can find. Is there any information you can gather about the world using a different kind of sense, beyond the "big five"?

TASTE:

❋ The Spring air
❋ A falling snowflake

FEEL:

❋ The Sun on your skin
❋ Rain on your face
❋ Your feet squelching in mud

OTHER:

❋ A sense of lightness
❋ Hope
❋ Increased energy, excitement

PLANTS & ANIMALS OF THE SEASON

Is it only us humans who recognize the return of light? Or do animals celebrate the Equinox, too? How about plants?

Yes! Of course they do!

The whole Earth celebrates the joy of longer days.

Listen: The birds are coming back ... cheeping, squawking, and hopping around looking for food.

Look: The ground is softening, and bulbs push their way up through the dirt as it thaws, toward the sunlight. Buds, tightly clenched, are preparing to unfurl.

HARES

For most of the year, hares are nocturnal, but around the time of the Spring Equinox, they come out to mate. Unlike their rabbit cousins who live in burrows underground, hares build nest-like homes by flattening tall grass. Sometimes a ground-nesting bird will take over a hare's nest and lay its eggs there, which may explain the legend of the Easter bunny—a bunny who carries a basket of colorful eggs!

RABBITS

Rabbits are CREPUSCULAR creatures, which means they are most active around dawn and dusk—the in-between times. If you go out to watch the sunrise or the sunset around the Equinox, you may come across one hopping around, even in the city.

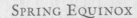
SNAKES

Like the feathered serpent of Kukulkan
in Chichen Itza, the snake is an animal of the Equinox
because it shows us how to shed our Winter shell and get
comfortable in our new skin—acknowledging that as we
do so, we may feel a bit raw at first. Remember, no
matter how we may change on the outside, we
each carry something powerful and constant,
deep within.

BIRDS

The more you listen to the birds, the better
you'll be able to recognize their calls. Eventually,
you may find you can even understand what
they're communicating!

See if you can befriend a bird. It helps to
have a pocket full of nuts or seeds. Start off by
scattering your treats from a distance. Come
back every day to the same place, at the same
time, and the birds may learn to trust you. With
enough time and patience, you might be blessed
by a bird landing on you, maybe even eating out
of your hand!

On Encountering Death

Even though we're looking for signs of life, when out on Ostara walks, we may come across death. If you live in a place that gets snow, it's likely to be melting now, and the thaw lets loose smells of decay that have been frozen over in Winter. Finding a dead animal can be shocking or sad. It can be helpful to stand (or crouch down) over the body and say a few words. For example:

Goodbye, dear bird (squirrel, mouse, etc.).
May you be in peace and may Spring's golden light
carry you through the next stages of the cycle.

Be careful not to touch the animal, as it's returning to the earth where its body will bring nutrients to the soil and help new life to grow. The DECOMPOSITION process involves MICROORGANISMS that, though invisible to our human eyes, can make us very sick if we touch them and get them inside our bodies.

Spring can be painful, as joyful as it is. Sometimes Spring carries with it the sorrow of our losses over Winter. It's important not to run too quickly from what we've just been through. This is what's called a LIMINAL time—a sort of in-between stage, a time of transition. Often, death and birth stand side by side.

PLANTING YOUR GARDEN

The Spring Equinox is an ideal time to start your seeds so that, come Summer, your plants will be large, healthy, and hardy. Think about what you want to grow. Flowers? Herbs? A small herb garden is a good place to start. If you don't have space outside, you can grow plants in pots inside by a window.

You will need:

❀ Seed packets
❀ Small paper cups
❀ Soil
❀ Spray bottle of water
❀ Popsicle sticks
❀ Pen or marker

1. Research what your particular plants need. Most herbs actually prefer sandy, well-draining soil. Some need a sunny spot, while others are happier in the shade.

2. Fill your cups with soil and follow the instructions on the back of the seed packets. You'll want to mist your dirt with the spray bottle to keep it moist, but don't overdo it or your soil may grow mold.

3. Using a pen or marker, label your popsicle sticks with the names of the herbs you've planted. Place each in its corresponding cup. (If you don't have popsicle sticks, you can label your paper cups directly.)

Suggestions for a first herb garden:

The following herbs are easy to care for and make delightful teas, as they all possess calm, energizing properties and are quite tasty:

Chamomile, lemon balm, mint, tulsi/holy basil, oregano

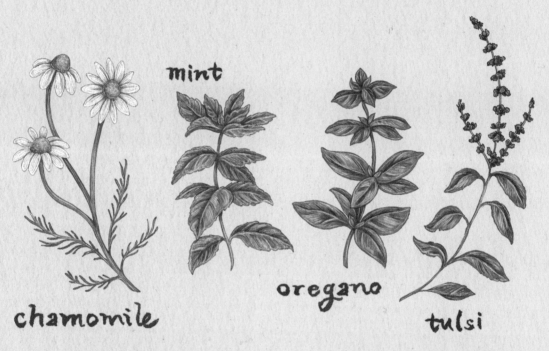

mint

chamomile

oregano

tulsi

Some other herbs are harder to start from seed but are readily available at most plant nurseries or hardware stores. They grow quite nicely in pots and planters, too. Once big enough to harvest from, they make lovely ingredients in breads, scrambled eggs, and other meals, as well as refreshing and soothing additions to a hot bath:

Rosemary, lavender, thyme, marjoram

PSSSt — Did you know you can talk to your seedlings? Who knows? Maybe if you listen closely, they'll even answer!

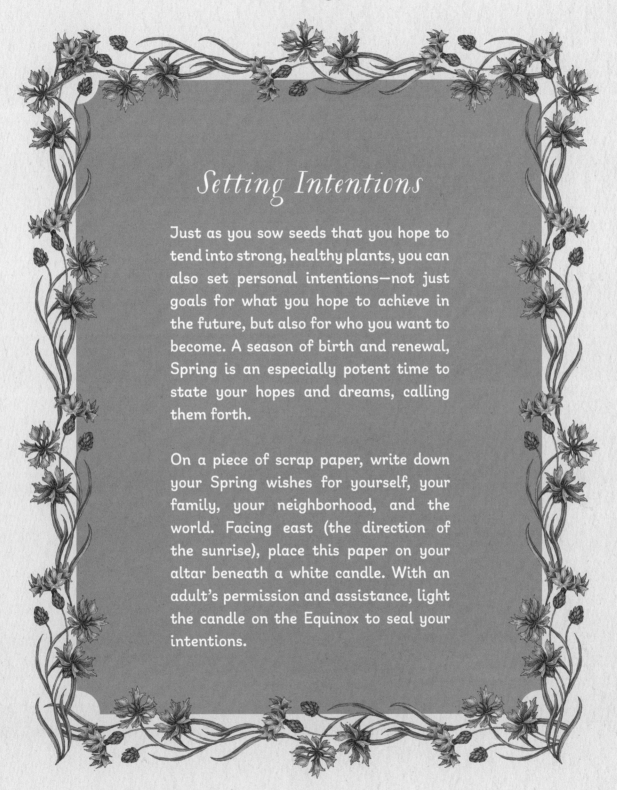

Setting Intentions

Just as you sow seeds that you hope to tend into strong, healthy plants, you can also set personal intentions—not just goals for what you hope to achieve in the future, but also for who you want to become. A season of birth and renewal, Spring is an especially potent time to state your hopes and dreams, calling them forth.

On a piece of scrap paper, write down your Spring wishes for yourself, your family, your neighborhood, and the world. Facing east (the direction of the sunrise), place this paper on your altar beneath a white candle. With an adult's permission and assistance, light the candle on the Equinox to seal your intentions.

ALTAR BUILDING

An ALTAR is a place of personal, symbolic significance and power, often spiritual in nature. Windowsills are a good place to set up an altar, but the corner of a desk or the top of your dresser can also work well. Any flat surface will do, so long as it won't be disturbed when you're not around.

First, place a piece of pretty cloth down to designate the space, then add objects that represent the themes and qualities you want in your life.

A rock may signify calm or groundedness, for example; flowers represent love, beauty, and abundance. As you find special items on your walks, you may feel called to place them on your altar to remind you of the peace and connection you find outside. (Just be careful not to disturb any plants or critters as you do this.)

If there's an animal you identify with, or whose characteristics you want to embody—a tiger's bravery, for instance, or a dog's loyalty—find a figurine or a picture of one to put on your altar. Many people put photos of their ANCESTORS on their altars to memorialize, honor, or communicate with them. In some cultures, it's customary to leave offerings for them, like a cookie or a piece of candy, especially if there was some treat they especially enjoyed while alive. Keep in mind that the word "ancestor" can mean different things to different people. Often, it refers to our older family members who have died, but you could also think of a rock, tree, or mushroom as your ancestor. All beings—living and dead—are related, even if not by blood.

Remember that there is no right or wrong way to make an altar. The most important things to bring to it are care and intention. Your altar can be a space to celebrate things you find beautiful, or it can be where you collect your strength and confidence. It might be a place of prayer, whatever that looks like for you, or a spot where you sit and are still with your thoughts and feelings.

However you use it, your altar is something to tend and return to. Throughout the course of the year, it changes and grows with you and with the seasons.

Suggestions for a Spring Equinox altar: A decorated egg, feathers, seeds, a bowl of fresh water, daffodils or other early bulb flowers, a white candle

Colors to include: Pastel yellow, green, white, pink, light blue

Visiting your altar with an open mind may help remind you that you're not alone, and that you can always find guidance. Often, the best answers come from within.

MORE RITUALS FOR OSTARA

SUNRISE & SUNSET

On the morning of the Equinox, wake up in time to face due east and watch the Sun come up. Observe the way the colors gradually change. Observe the intensity of the light. If the Equinox itself is overcast or rainy, you might want to wait for a clear morning for full effect. Try to stay silent and keep your mind free of thoughts; this way, you can find out what the sunrise makes you feel.

Later, try the same with the sunset!

If you live in a city that's built on a grid—one with mostly straight streets that run north to south and east to west—you can experience a modern-day henge-like spectacle, just by going downtown before sunset and facing west. The tall buildings stand as majestic as the megaliths of the past, and the golden rays blazing through the corridors shine with as much intensity and mystery as if you were in an ancient setting.

If you live in a more rural or suburban place, you can still take time to watch the sunset in a moment of silent meditation, with loved ones, or by yourself—though you may realize as you sit that you're never *really* alone.

Set an alarm! At the time of the Equinox, the sun comes up between 7:00 and 7:30 a.m., and it goes down between 7:00 and 7:30 p.m.

Neighborhood Cleanup

If you live in a place with snowy winters, once the snow starts melting, you'll probably notice a lot of litter in your neighborhood streets and parks. You can do something about it!

You will need:
* Garbage bags
* Rubber gloves

Call up a couple friends or grab a family member, and go out and pick up some garbage! Believe it or not, hunting and gathering trash can be a lot of fun, not to mention a kind service to the local wildlife. Sometimes, neighborhoods organize big cleaning events that you can join, especially around Earth Day (April 22), but there's no reason you can't do it anytime you see a need. Just make sure to wear rubber gloves and wash your hands very well when you get home. Never pick up anything sharp!

Making Peace

The people of the Altai Mountain region of Siberia traditionally take the days around the Spring Equinox to make peace with all. What a beautiful way to celebrate, and what a useful ritual! Just as we might clean and repair our home at this time of year, we can make the same effort to mend our personal relationships.

Is there anybody you're quarreling with? Perhaps you can make your best effort to resolve it, so that you can enter the new season without conflict. Imagine the spirit of forgiveness washing over your body like a fresh Spring breeze. Take a deep breath in and fill your body with this clean air. Using this energy, send the person you've been fighting with wishes of peace and joy. Think about what else it will take to heal the situation, and whether that's something you can or want to take on at this moment.

MAKE YOUR OWN MAGIC WAND

The Spring Equinox is a powerful time for intention-setting or wish-making. Sometimes just saying something out loud makes it more real. A wand is a tool that can extend your reach and influence when releasing your personal intentions into the world.

You will need:
* The right stick
* *Optional:* Paint or markers; ribbons; crystals, acorns, stones, and/or feathers; a hot glue gun (be sure an adult helps you with this tool!)

1. Begin by looking for a stick. You'll know the right one when you see it. It's best to find a stick that's fallen on its own, rather than snapping or cutting one from a living tree. It's nice to thank the tree for the gift, too.

2. You can paint your wand, decorate it with ribbons, or glue things to it—whatever feels right. The important thing is to make the wand *yours*.

How will you use your wand? To encourage your plants to grow? To help with homework? To build your confidence? Keep in mind that whatever energy you put out into the world usually comes back to you, one way or another.

RITUAL BATH: A SPRING SHOWER

One way to symbolically mark new beginnings is to clean your body. This time of year is often rather rainy, so for this spoke of the Wheel, a shower might feel more appropriate than a bath. You can also make a simple potion to slough off old, dead skin cells and leave yourself feeling fresh, smooth, and rejuvenated—ready for anything.

You will need:

* A mixing bowl
* A spoon or spatula
* 1 cup sugar (brown or cane)
* ½ cup coconut, olive, or almond oil
* *Optional:* A lemon or orange; a grater

1. In a mixing bowl, combine the sugar and oil, stirring it with a spoon or spatula until well blended.

2. If you want your scrub to have a refreshing citrus scent, carefully scrape an unpeeled lemon or orange against a grater to make some zest. Add it to the sugar and oil mixture and stir it all together.

3. Before entering the shower, reflect on what you no longer want in your life—things you want to let go of. Perhaps you want to shed a particular habit, thought, or feeling that has been causing you stress lately.

4. Bring your sugar scrub with you into the shower. Think of the things you wish to shed as you take a scoop of your potion and gently rub it over your body, avoiding the face and any sensitive areas. As you rinse, imagine those things washing away down the drain. Let the warm water flow over your head and body.

To maximize your magic, sing a song while you wash!

BELTANE

MAY 1

in the Northern Hemisphere

NOVEMBER 1

in the Southern Hemisphere

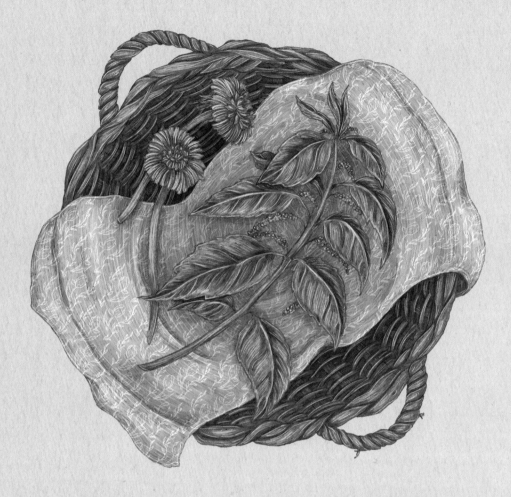

RHYTHM OF THE WHEEL

Beltane, or May Day, falls at the midway point between the Spring Equinox and Summer Solstice. These days that fall between the Equinoxes and the Solstices are called cross-quarter days, and often, they're celebrated with just as much ritual and excitement.

SPIRIT OF THE SEASON

Beltane is a time of increase: as the days continue to lengthen, flora and fauna grow and multiply.

This holiday is all about Life.

It's a celebration of all bodies in and on Earth: plant, insect, mammal, bird, reptile, tree, microorganism. On Beltane, we enjoy and explore what it means to be alive: to breathe, to circulate, to process, to move.

This time of year, everything grows so quickly you can practically watch it happen. Fields unfurl into vibrant rainbow carpets. Trees are tipped with neon green fluff and delicate lace blossoms. Eggs crack open, and ducklings and goslings parade behind their parents.

The fresh breeze carries a confidence that the Sun is here to stay. We've crossed the threshold and left Winter behind. The birds' noisy chirps are an umbrella of sound before sunrise, signaling their return as they call out for old friends, maybe hoping to make some new ones. The energy of the world is high and lively, like a merry party. Animals scamper in search of dance partners; flowers of every color burst open in bloom. The Earth is fully awake, in an explosion of color, sounds, and smells.

COME CELEBRATE THIS SEASON WITH THE REST OF EARTH'S INHABITANTS!

GET YOUR BLOOD FLOWING

Clench your fists as tight as you can, directing all your force down into your hands. Imagine your hands are buds, tightly wrapped. Now, slowly relax them. Uncurl your fingers, like they are flower petals gently opening. Continue to stretch your fingers out as far as they will go, expanding your strength and energy outwards.

You might notice that, like the squirrels and birds, you have more energy at this time of year. It's more comfortable to be outside, the Sun is shining longer, and the breeze is fresh and warm. Take advantage of your energy and start moving! Even if you're still feeling a little sluggish, go outside, stretch, and get your heart pounding. Go on a bike ride, dance, run; do some pushups, some jumping jacks, or challenge a friend to a jump-rope contest—whatever is within your ability.

As you move around, causing your blood to circulate throughout your body, new ideas are likely to start flowing, too. Stoke that creative fire with some physical movement!

HARNESS YOUR CREATIVITY

The world looks like a painting this time of year; color and life are everywhere. This *joie de vivre* (a French phrase meaning "joy of living") can flow right into you, if you let it!

Take your journal and some colored pencils to your favorite green space, and try to render some of the leaves, petals, and creatures you see. Drawing can be an expression of love, following the lines and forms of a thing and trying to replicate them. If you feel more in the mood to just scribble colors onto the page, though, that's fine, too. Don't be too concerned with the outcome of your drawings. It's more about enjoying the feeling of making your mark.

LOOK OUT FOR MISCHIEF!

Beltane is alive with joy, but an unpredictable streak of mischief also charges the air. Samhain (Halloween) is directly across the Wheel, and as we say on that holiday, *the veil is thin* at this time of year, too (more on page 147). Historically, people have noticed a tendency for the uncanny to occur—strange coincidences popping up all over the place. The living creatures of Earth are wide awake and scurrying around, and some claim to have encountered fairies amidst all the hubbub. But beware: the wee folk are more likely to play tricks than grant wishes!

If you want, you can leave a small cup of milk or a lump of bread for the fairies. Find a hole in a tree in your park or yard and nestle your gift in there to win the fairies' goodwill (or at least to deflect their mischief!).

PSSST Legend has it that washing your face with Beltane dew—dew collected on the morning of May 1—will make you as beautiful on the outside as you are on the inside. Take that as you will!

CELEBRATIONS: PAST & PRESENT

BELTANE

Beltane means "Bright Fire" in Old Irish, because in Celtic tradition, this holiday was a fire festival. DRUIDS were in charge of lighting giant bonfires on the tops of hills in Irish herding communities. Farmers would lead their cattle around the fires in a ritual that was meant to protect their animals from disease. Then they would move their livestock into fresh Summer pastures. Beyond the magical aspects of this tradition, the heat from the blaze likely burned off disease-causing pests, hence the idea that fire has cleansing powers.

Druids

In Ancient Celtic culture, druids were highly revered SHAMANS: people who served as communicators between nature, the spirit world, and other humans. Their main teaching was REINCARNATION: the idea that souls are immortal and do not perish, but after death pass into a new form. The druids were well versed in the wisdom of plants, animals, and the stars. When the Romans, and later the Christians, invaded Celtic territory, the druids were considered dangerous and were killed. To retain secrecy, the druids created their own tree language called Ogham, carving their knowledge into wood and stone.

FLORALIA

The ancient Roman festival of flowers began on April 28 and lasted one week, celebrated more by common people than by the upper classes. People dressed in their brightest colors; games and theatrical performances abounded in honor of Flora, goddess of flowers and vegetation. Goats and hares were released into the crowds, adding to the atmosphere of chaos and fun. One year, there was even a tightrope-walking elephant!

MAY DAY

In some Germanic and British regions, people continue the age-old tradition of gathering outside to decorate and dance around a maypole. A tall post is installed in the ground with multicolored ribbons tied to the top. People grab a ribbon and weave in, out, and around the pole to the sound of drums, laughter, and song. Afterwards, a feast is shared. People wear flower wreaths upon their heads, and a May Queen is crowned. May Day is also sometimes known as the Great Wedding: animals pair off and love warms the air!

MAIUMA

The ancient Greek festival of Maiuma was a celebration of the victory of life over death, and honored Aphrodite, goddess of love, and Dionysus, god of wine. Wild banquets and theatrical performances would often last all night long, the streets lit with torches to keep the party going. The revelry was so rowdy that eventually Emperor Constantine outlawed all Maiuma festivities.

HANAMI

Each year, there's a brief window of time in which to admire the beauty of the *sakura,* or cherry blossoms, in Japan. Trees are topped with soft, fluffy clouds of pale pink flowers, and people come from near and far to witness their beauty. The experience is all the more special because the blossoms only last for about a week before they flutter to the ground and turn brown. The holiday of Hanami is a reminder of EPHEMERALITY: the idea that nothing is permanent, so we ought to appreciate what we have while it's with us.

INTERNATIONAL WORKERS DAY

On May 1, 1886, thousands of workers in Chicago, tired of being overworked and underpaid, gathered in Haymarket Square to protest how badly they were being treated by their bosses. They refused to go into their factory jobs, proving they were essential and their rights and needs could not continue to be ignored. "Eight hours for work, eight hours for rest, eight hours for what we will!" they demanded.

Sadly, the protest turned violent as police tried to force the workers to go home. Eleven people died, and hundreds more were injured. But the fight for fairness for workers didn't end. Because of the workers' activism, the weekend was established. In many countries the world over, the value of workers is honored on May 1, a day for acknowledging and feeling SOLIDARITY—a sense of unity or shared interest.

8 hours for work

8 hours for what we will

8 hours for rest

SCAVENGER HUNT

What flowers grow where you live?

Learn as many of their names as you can. Learn their scientific names, their indigenous names, their nicknames. Give them new names you make up yourself!

Try to find the full rainbow of colors in the flowers.

Draw and/or name them in your journal. If you have chalk pastels or watercolor paints, try to replicate their shades as you find them.

Dandelions! Violets! Magnolias! Lilacs!

Go Deeper: Learn the smells of different flowers. Teach yourself to identify plants by their scents! Test yourself, or a friend, and discover how discerning your nose can be.

Cherry Blossoms, Apple Blossoms, Tulips! Red Buds, Bluebells, Crocuses!

A SPECTRUM is a way to organize things—defining something by placing it in context with other things around it. Notice that the colors of many flowers fall in between categories. Blue-green? Red-orange? That's pretty normal for a spectrum. The closer you examine the colors, the more complex you realize they are; sometimes it's hard to classify them into distinct categories. Plus, as time passes, the color of the flower might change, and it could end up in a different place on the spectrum. That's all fine! A color doesn't have to fit exactly inside of one box to be beautiful.

PLANTS OF THE SEASON

In the Garden

Spring is really here! Outside, you'll see plants bolting up, their leaves thickening. If you planted seeds during Spring Equinox and everything went as hoped, you'll have a tray full of green seedlings you can transfer into bigger pots or into the ground. If you don't have seedlings, don't worry; you can still DIRECT SOW: if you have some space in your yard, or in a school or community garden, you can plant seeds straight into the dirt. And if that's not an option, it's not too late to buy a starter from a plant nursery, hardware store, or grocery store.

When sprouts first pop up, they mostly look the same, but once they get their first true leaves, notice how different they are from one another! Some are round and waxy, others are delicate and feathery, and still others grow wide and rough.

> *Did You Know?* The month of May is named after Greek
> goddess Maia, nurse and nurturer. Spring Equinox was
> about planning and putting down first seeds. Now, during
> Beltane, we've entered the season of tending. Tending
> means caring. It means loving, which in large part means
> noticing and listening. Just as we must tend our garden
> with care, we must tend to ourselves, and each other.

Your plants will require daily attention as they grow. You'll have to water them. You may have to weed, plucking out the sprouts that try to compete with your herbs for space and nutrients. Your plants might appreciate some COMPOST, too.

IN THE WILD

FORAGING means gathering plants from where they spring up on their own. It's an ancient practice of all peoples (and many animals!) around the world, and there's no better way to discover how generous our Earth truly is. Even in cities, nourishing plants grow all over the place!

However, it's very important to forage carefully because some plants have poisonous look-alikes. Just as many plants have the power to heal and nourish, some can be toxic.

Follow these tips and review the safety notes on pages viii-ix:

- Consult more than one resource when identifying plants: You might start with an app like iNaturalist, or a field guide for your area. Next, ask a knowledgeable adult for help.

- Never take from someone's private property without their permission.

- Be respectful and don't take more than you can use. Watch for eggs or cocoons on the undersides of leaves and let those plants be.

- Avoid areas where dogs may have peed or pooped in the grass.

It's a good habit to talk to the plants before and as you pick them. It might feel weird at first, but give it a try, and it'll start to feel natural in no time!

Hello, flower! Do you mind if I pick a few of you to make tea?

Pause and listen. See if you feel any kind of reply. Sometimes, you might receive a message about something you can do for the plant. Does it need water? Should you help scatter its seeds? If you decide to go ahead with gathering, don't forget to say thanks. The generosity of plants is something to honor and aspire to.

Violet Lemonade Potion

Makes: 1 *pitcher*

Making violet lemonade is a fantastic first foraging project because of the incredible transformation the violets undergo. There's no better word for it than magic! With their small purple faces, violets are easy to recognize, grow all over the place, and have no toxic look-alikes.

You will need:
❁ Wild violets
❁ 1 tablespoon sugar or honey
❁ ½ lemon

You will also need:
❁ Basket or bag
❁ Saucepot
❁ Wooden spoon
❁ Pitcher
❁ Sieve or strainer

1. Look for a patch of wild violets in a park or field in early Spring and fill a basket or bag with flowers. When you get home, wash the flowers and put them in a pot. Cover them with about an inch of water.

2. With an adult's help, use the stove to bring your flower-water mixture to a boil, then turn the heat to low and keep simmering about five minutes. The pigment in the flowers will break down and turn the water dark.

3. Remove the pot from heat, and add a tablespoon of honey or sugar. Stir with a wooden spoon and wait for the mixture to cool.

4. Filter out the flowers with a sieve and pour the mixture into a pitcher.

5. Squeeze the juice from the lemon into the pitcher and see for yourself what happens!

DANDELIONS
(Taraxacum officinale)

The dandelion is a small, sun-bright flower that can grow just about anywhere its seeds land. If there are dandelions in your park, that's a good sign there aren't a ton of harmful chemicals on the grass. If the soil does contain toxins deeper down, the dandelion sucks that poison out of the ground and stores it in its roots, cleaning the soil through its little body and making the area healthier. Its powerful roots also break up hard soil, loosening up the ground so more delicate plants can find a place to take root, too.

Among the first of Spring flowers to appear, dandelions provide some of the earliest sources of food for POLLINATORS.

Pollinators are insects, birds, and small mammals that travel from plant to plant, grabbing and exchanging pollen that allows plants to reproduce. If it weren't for these small helpers, many of our favorite flowers and vegetables wouldn't exist.

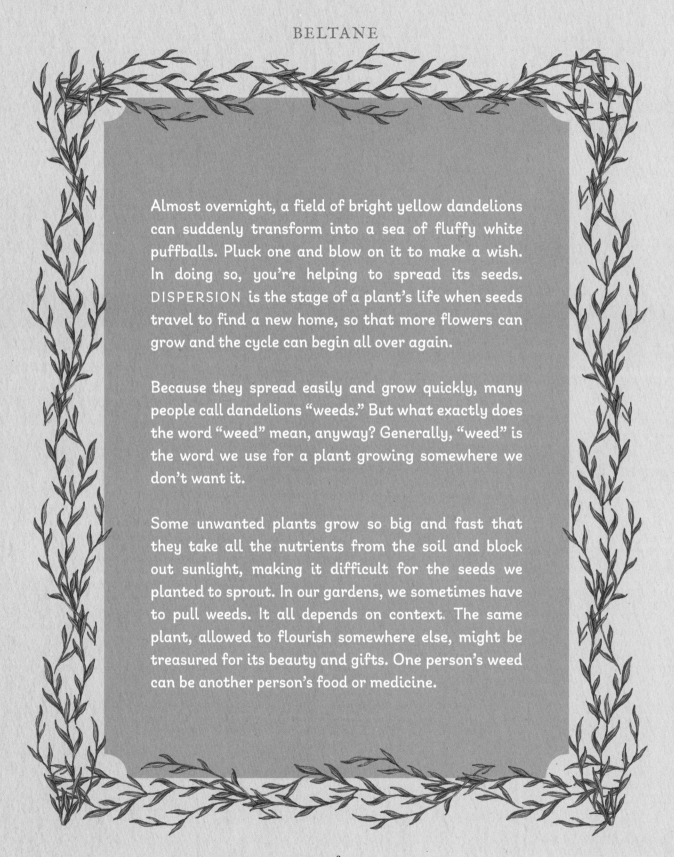

Almost overnight, a field of bright yellow dandelions can suddenly transform into a sea of fluffy white puffballs. Pluck one and blow on it to make a wish. In doing so, you're helping to spread its seeds. DISPERSION is the stage of a plant's life when seeds travel to find a new home, so that more flowers can grow and the cycle can begin all over again.

Because they spread easily and grow quickly, many people call dandelions "weeds." But what exactly does the word "weed" mean, anyway? Generally, "weed" is the word we use for a plant growing somewhere we don't want it.

Some unwanted plants grow so big and fast that they take all the nutrients from the soil and block out sunlight, making it difficult for the seeds we planted to sprout. In our gardens, we sometimes have to pull weeds. It all depends on context. The same plant, allowed to flourish somewhere else, might be treasured for its beauty and gifts. One person's weed can be another person's food or medicine.

DANDELION TEA

Go ahead and pick a handful of those furry gold flower heads. Remove the bitter green bases from the flowers and set them aside. Wash the blooms, place them into a cup, and cover with hot water. After about 10 minutes, strain out the flowers, add some honey, and enjoy! It's a great cleansing tonic.

Dandelion greens, once thoroughly washed, can also be eaten raw, in a salad, or cooked up with a little butter and a squeeze of lemon. Ask an adult to help you try this! Not only are dandelions tasty, they also make your body feel good because they provide many essential vitamins and minerals.

Not in the mood for tea?
Try making a
dandelion crown!

1.

2.

3.

4.

Dandelions are an ideal flower to forage because they grow so abundantly. It's unlikely you'll be disturbing the ecosystem—the living things in the area—by picking them. Even if you and a friend make crowns and drink dandelion tea, there will still be plenty for bugs and other pollinators to eat from.

BELTANE ALTAR

The world outside is bright and colorful, so bring some of that floral, joyful energy to your altar!

Displaying flowers on your altar is a way to honor their beauty, but be aware that when you harvest a flower, you are removing it from its natural ecosystem. Another option is to bring a potted plant to you altar. You could also decorate using fabric flowers or drawings and photos of your favorite blooms.

Suggested items:

- All things green, to encourage growth and expansion
- A green candle
- Houseplants
- A mini-maypole (a stick with different colored ribbons tied to it)
- Fairy-related charms or drawings

Colors to include: Vibrant hues, especially the blue of the sky; the green of grass; and the reds, purples, and golds of flowers.

During the Spring Equinox, you set intentions. Now, look back on those goals, and check in with how you feel about them. Are these still the things you want? Do you feel closer to having them? If not, that's okay. Beltane is a great time to recommit to your goals. It might be helpful to interview yourself about your wishes. What can you do to get to where you want to be? Is anything standing in your way?

Perhaps your plan needs some adjustment. Try to brainstorm new strategies you can try.

As the days continue to lengthen, open your heart to opportunity. Allow space to let in more of what you desire.

MORE RITUALS FOR BELTANE

CONNECTING TO NATURE

What do you think of when you hear the word *nature?*

Maybe you imagine a wild forest where no human has stepped foot for a long time. Maybe you think of flowers, animals, and trees. Do you think of people or cities when you hear the word *nature?*

In truth, we humans are nature, too. Despite historical attempts to control and distance ourselves from other living beings, the universe is a living thing, and we humans are but one aspect of this enormous, magical system.

For most of human existence, people have been connected to their environment, depending on it and giving back to it. It's only in more recent history that such stark lines have been drawn between humans and the Earth.

As a result, these days we might think of "Nature" as some grand, distant other, something to observe and visit.

But we don't have to think this way! The land we inhabit has experienced many changes. Try to find out the history of where you live and see how far back you can go. Research your neighborhood a hundred years ago, two hundred years ago, a thousand years ago—even further, if you can! Our Earth has been through a lot. But it is strong and resilient, and we can dedicate our lives to tending and repairing it, each other, and ourselves.

Since you are a part of nature, where you are *is* nature. That said, go ahead and find the dirt; find the green, the growing, the living. Speak to it. Listen to it. The very land you walk on is alive, teeming with life you can and cannot see.

City Greenspaces

You don't have to go to the woods to connect with nature. Look around where you live, and you'll find all kinds of living beings sharing the city with you: plants, pets, insects, animals, mushrooms, moss . . . not to mention the trillions of microorganisms that are all over everything, too small to see.

Here are some examples of places in the city where the presence of other living things may be easier to find and connect with:

Parks, boulevards, empty lots,
playgrounds, yards, cemeteries, courtyards

Make sure you are respectful of the places you visit, always leaving them the same as or better than you found them. As you build your bond with others—human and non—you'll find yourself tapping into the great well of magic that is our universe.

Is an empty lot really "empty"? What's living there?

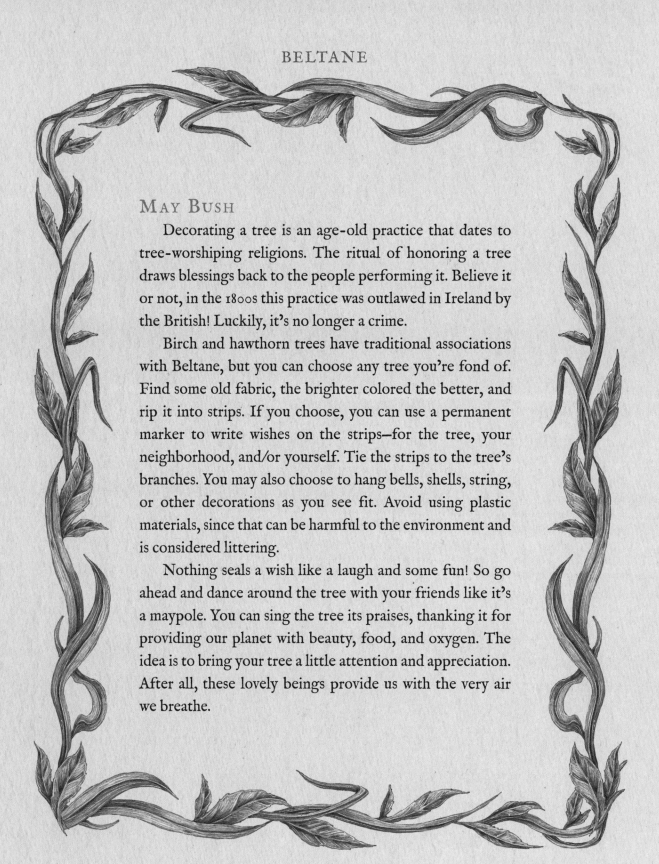

MAY BUSH

Decorating a tree is an age-old practice that dates to tree-worshiping religions. The ritual of honoring a tree draws blessings back to the people performing it. Believe it or not, in the 1800s this practice was outlawed in Ireland by the British! Luckily, it's no longer a crime.

Birch and hawthorn trees have traditional associations with Beltane, but you can choose any tree you're fond of. Find some old fabric, the brighter colored the better, and rip it into strips. If you choose, you can use a permanent marker to write wishes on the strips—for the tree, your neighborhood, and/or yourself. Tie the strips to the tree's branches. You may also choose to hang bells, shells, string, or other decorations as you see fit. Avoid using plastic materials, since that can be harmful to the environment and is considered littering.

Nothing seals a wish like a laugh and some fun! So go ahead and dance around the tree with your friends like it's a maypole. You can sing the tree its praises, thanking it for providing our planet with beauty, food, and oxygen. The idea is to bring your tree a little attention and appreciation. After all, these lovely beings provide us with the very air we breathe.

Pressed Flower Bookmark

The beauty of a living blossom is short-lived, but if you press flowers, you can keep their memory alive longer. If you planted wildflowers during the Spring Equinox, or you find some growing in the park, you can pick a few to preserve—as long as there are plenty of others around for the pollinators.

You will need:

- ❀ Flowers
- ❀ Thick, heavy hardbound books
- ❀ Cardstock paper
- ❀ Scissors
- ❀ Clear packing tape
- ❀ *Optional:* A holepunch, ribbon

1. Place the flowers you've picked between the pages of a thick, hardbound book, then put the book back on the shelf for a week or two, wedged tight between other books. When you next open the pages, you'll find a paper-thin surprise!

2. Cut a piece of cardstock paper into a strip about as tall as your favorite book and as wide as the packing tape.

3. Arrange your pressed flowers onto the paper in a way that pleases your eye.

4. Lay the tape down along the paper, wrapping it around so both sides are laminated. If you want, you can use a holepunch at the top and tie a ribbon or two through the hole.

Ritual Bath: Sunbathing

On a sunny day, warm enough that you don't need a jacket, find a patch of grass and lie down.

Remember how Beltane is a fire holiday, and that fire has cleansing properties? The Sun is a great big fireball in the sky, and it can feel nourishing to let its rays wash over your body—especially after a long winter.

Try to choose a breezy day, so you can experience the soothing sensation of the wind caressing your relaxed body while you soak up the sunshine. Close your eyes and enjoy your body at peace. Concentrate on the breath flowing in and out of your lungs. Imagine you're a plant, gathering energy from the Sun's light. Notice the sounds you hear around you. Allow your body to melt into its surroundings.

Remember: The sun is fire, and fire can burn.
Be sure to apply sunscreen with a high SPF and limit
your sunbath to no more than twenty minutes.

MIDSUMMER:
Summer Solstice

JUNE 21

in the Northern Hemisphere

DECEMBER 21

in the Southern Hemisphere

RHYTHM OF THE WHEEL

We have arrived at the ZENITH of the solar calendar, the very peak! Summer Solstice is high noon in the Wheel of the Year: the longest day, with the most hours of light stretching between sunrise and sunset. Half the Earth is tilted dramatically toward the Sun, basking in its glow, and that side of the globe blossoms and blooms. The other side, of course, is tilted far from the Sun, experiencing the long, cold nights of Winter—and that's where we'll be in six months, when the Wheel has turned.

The word SOLSTICE comes from Latin words meaning "sun" and "stand still." For a few days before and after Solstice, it seems like the Sun stays in the same position on the horizon—its highest point of the year.

That incredible, life-giving star!

Around the globe, Summer Solstice has long been a day to celebrate the Sun in its full glory.

SPIRIT OF THE SEASON

Full Bloom

The trees are topped in shaggy, green coats, providing cool, comforting shade. Plants have grown tall, their leaves full and thick, hiding all kinds of life in, on, and under their lush foliage. When you go for a walk in the park or the woods, how many shades of green can you see? It's amazing, really, how much variety exists within a single color.

When you recognize a plant and can name it, it's like saying hi to a friend. Once you're able to identify local plants, walking in the park sometimes feels like going to a party!

Solstice is often a time of bounty and abundance, of pure vitality. New flowers surround us with tantalizing scents and color; fruits form, grow, ripen, and glisten. This is *Summer*. The days are long, free, and open. Bees, birds, and butterflies flutter about. At night, if you're lucky, you can watch fireflies glow, lighting the sky with magic. Earth delights in a full expression of life, and so shall we.

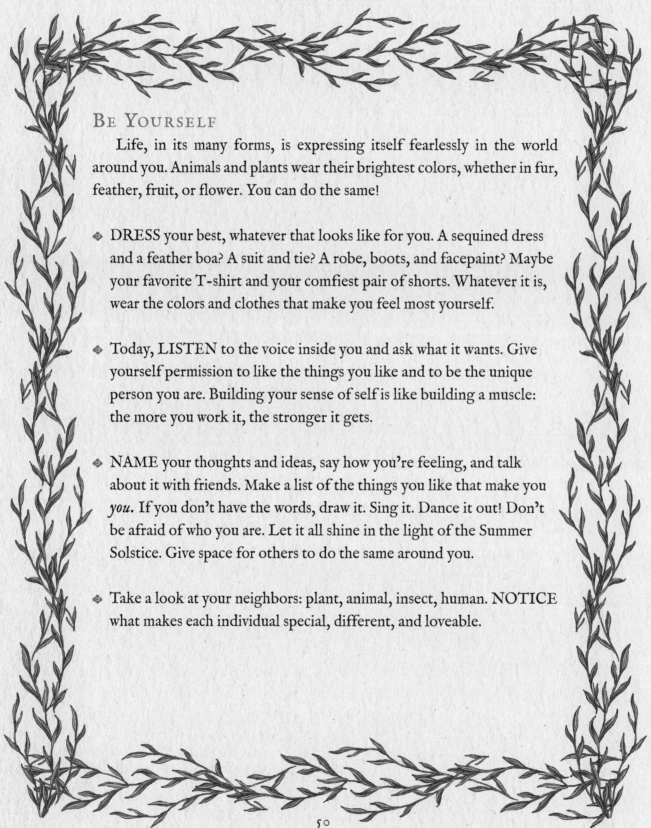

Be Yourself

Life, in its many forms, is expressing itself fearlessly in the world around you. Animals and plants wear their brightest colors, whether in fur, feather, fruit, or flower. You can do the same!

- DRESS your best, whatever that looks like for you. A sequined dress and a feather boa? A suit and tie? A robe, boots, and facepaint? Maybe your favorite T-shirt and your comfiest pair of shorts. Whatever it is, wear the colors and clothes that make you feel most yourself.

- Today, LISTEN to the voice inside you and ask what it wants. Give yourself permission to like the things you like and to be the unique person you are. Building your sense of self is like building a muscle: the more you work it, the stronger it gets.

- NAME your thoughts and ideas, say how you're feeling, and talk about it with friends. Make a list of the things you like that make you *you*. If you don't have the words, draw it. Sing it. Dance it out! Don't be afraid of who you are. Let it all shine in the light of the Summer Solstice. Give space for others to do the same around you.

- Take a look at your neighbors: plant, animal, insect, human. NOTICE what makes each individual special, different, and loveable.

CHANGE YOUR POINT OF VIEW.

Curiosity is one of our greatest assets in life. Testing things out from a new angle is a useful trick that can make you smarter and kinder. Besides, shaking things up can spark new ideas. You never know what you might learn, looking at something from a different perspective. It also happens to be one of many things *kids* tend to do better than grown-ups!

On the following pages, you'll find some ideas for how you might experiment with a different point of view.

CLIMB A TREE

Make sure you listen to the tree for the best, strongest footholds so neither of you gets hurt. How high can you go? What do you see, and how does it make you feel? Have a grown-up nearby while you test your boundaries. Will you climb down or jump?

TURN UPSIDE-DOWN

Can you do a handstand? Give it a try! If you keep flopping over, kick your legs up a tree or wall for a little extra support. Some people can even train themselves to walk on their hands. In yoga, upside-down poses are called INVERSIONS, and getting the heart above the head is said to have many benefits, like building confidence and increasing strength, energy, and balance.

WIDE-ANGLE VISION

Predators' eyes tend to be closer together and at the front of their face because they need sharp focus to home in on their prey in a sneak attack.

Prey animals, however, need a broader view so they can detect sudden movements that might mean danger. Their eyes tend to be farther apart, positioned toward the sides of their face.

Practicing wide-angle vision can help you see the world a little differently.

* Face forward with your arms in front of you.
* Wiggle your fingers.
* Be aware of the wiggling but look past your fingers.
* Let your vision go out of focus.
* Start moving your arms apart from one another, out to the sides, continuing to wiggle your fingers.

This exercise builds your PERIPHERAL VISION—your vision of what's on either side of you. Eventually, you'll be able to shift into wide-angle vision without the finger-wiggling. Your vision will blur as you lose focus, but you'll become more aware of movement within your range of sight.

Take Away One of Your Senses

Go on a walk through the park with a friend, keeping your eyes closed the whole time. If you find yourself sneaking peeks, tie a piece of fabric over your eyes as a blindfold. What different things do you notice when you aren't relying on your sense of vision? Alternatively, get a pair of earplugs or borrow a set of noise-canceling earmuffs and walk a familiar route with a trusted friend. Even the places we know well can seem new when we change our perspective!

Walk Silently

This exercise is about experimenting with your impact on the world, more than your perception of it. The goal is to be aware of your movement, trying to be as quiet as possible.

* Be aware of your breath.
* Listen and look at your surroundings before taking a step.
* Gently place the outside pad of one foot on the ground.
* Roll the pad down toward the big toe, lowering your weight onto that foot.
* Drop the heel.
* Repeat with the other foot.

It takes practice, but eventually, it can become second nature to walk silently. Test yourself by asking a friend to sit with their eyes closed at a distance from you. See how close you can get before they notice you! It's trickier walking across uneven ground and through bushes, so if you have a chance, try this in the woods.

CELEBRATIONS: PAST & PRESENT

THE GREAT PYRAMIDS AT GIZA

In ancient Egypt, Summer Solstice was a time for rejoicing as the rains flooded the Nile River, which in turn soaked and nourished the surrounding lands, allowing crops to flourish. For people completely dependent on the land for their food, this abundance was indeed something to praise.

To this day, the Sun sets between the pyramids on the Summer Solstice, the mysterious Sphinx resting between them, gazing out across the horizon.

THE GREAT SERPENT MOUND

An enormous grass-mound snake slithers and coils across almost two thousand feet of land: an earthwork built by the ancient Adena people of the Ohio River Valley. At one end, its open-mouthed head faces the Summer Solstice sunset. At the other, its tail spirals three times, aligning with the Winter Solstice sunrise and the two equinoxes. The twists of this enormous snake's body are thought to coincide with significant phases of the moon (for more on lunar phases, see page 187).

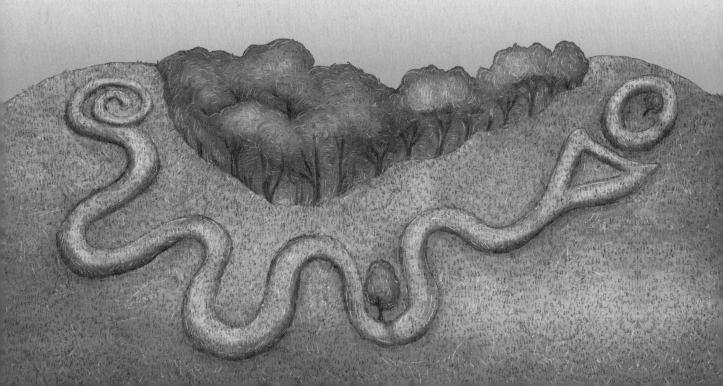

MIDSOMMAR OR JUHANNUS

Because Winter is especially long and dark the farther north you go, the Scandinavian countries of Sweden and Finland do their best to make the most of the Summer days. People tend to leave the cities to enjoy outdoor celebrations in the country—fishing, swimming, and boating; lighting bonfires; and eating foods like pickled herring and berries topped with cream.

ST. JOHN OF THE BAYOU

For over three hundred years, millions of people were kidnapped from Africa and forced to work in violent conditions in the U.S. The enslaved people weren't allowed to practice their beliefs. They found some ways to secretly maintain their traditions, however. In New Orleans, Louisiana, for example, many wove the Yoruba practices of their West African homeland together with Native American beliefs and the Catholic faith of their captors, developing the religion of Vodou.

Vodou priestess Marie Laveau (1801-1881) held an annual river baptism on the Summer Solstice, called St. John of the Bayou or St. John's Night. To this day, practitioners dress in all white and wash their heads in the bayou before feasting outside, while musicians play jazz and sing gospel songs. This celebration, and St. John's Night festivities in other places, are a testament to the resourcefulness and resilience of the people's magic.

FÊTE DE LA MUSIQUE

Over a thousand cities across the world have declared June 21 to be Make Music Day, or Fête de la Musique, a time to promote local musicians performing in public places. If you live in a city, go check out some free live music—or if you'd rather, make your own!

MAKE MUSIC!

When people gather to create something together
and the energy is really flowing, the whole becomes
greater than the sum of its parts. It's magic!

You don't have to be trained in music to have a good time making
songs with others. Pots, pans, and spoons can be drums, and your
voice is an instrument you take with you wherever you go.

To make a simple percussion instrument, you will need:

* A straight stick, about 10 inches long and ½ inch thick (slightly longer and thicker than a pencil)
* A metal file
* Another, smaller stick

With an adult's supervision, use the file to carve six to
eight notches into the bigger stick, about a pinky-
finger's distance apart. You want the grooves to go
about halfway through the stick. When you're
satisfied with the number of notches, take the
smaller stick and run it down the big stick.
Up and down: there you go . . . rhythm
section! Play with the sounds as you
strike it, and above all, have fun!

Earth-Body Artwork

In her work, Cuban-American artist Ana Mendieta explored the presence of the human form and spirit in relation to its environment. She didn't use paint or pencils to make art; she used her body and the world around it, imprinting and marking her form into cracked clay, tall grasses, flowers, leaves, water, and more. Her work is haunting, reminding us—without using words—of humanity's impact on and connection to the animal and spirit realms.

Perhaps you can experiment with leaving your temporary mark, using material you find in the world around you. Try tracing your shadow or finding a way to leave your footprint. Be mindful you cause no harm to the space, and never change it in any permanent way. Think about your relationship to your environment, and how it changes over time. Consider how, or if, you want to document your art before it disappears on its own.

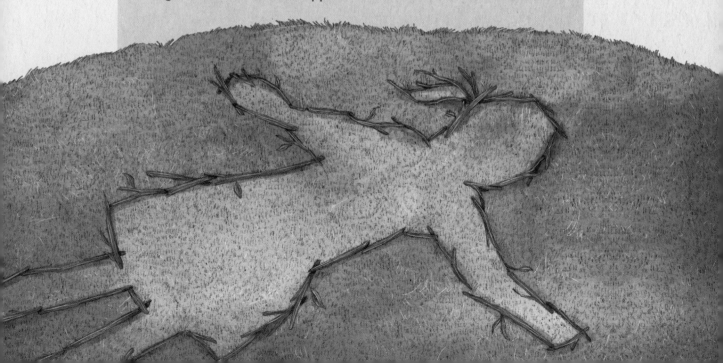

SCAVENGER HUNT

THE GREEN MAN

Usually depicted as a wood spirit with leaves and vegetation growing from his tangled hair, the Green Man is a quiet, kindly presence that watches over the life of a forest, or in more urban settings, the park or boulevards. If your city has old buildings downtown, you may be able to find a Green Man carved into stone, looking down on traffic. Versions of the wild woodsman ARCHETYPE appear in stories from Iraq, India, Haiti, Ireland, and more.

An ARCHETYPE is a spirit or character who appears in many cultures, representing a deep truth of human experience.

The Green Man is considered a bridge between human civilization and the wilderness beyond. He's a protector of nature but is known to cause mischief, and in some places, he serves as a warning. Usually, he's only ever spotted out of the corner of an eye before he quickly disappears behind a tree.

Once you start looking for faces in trees and bushes, you may start seeing them everywhere. The scientific name for this phenomenon is PAREIDOLIA, the human tendency to see faces wherever we look. But a scientific explanation doesn't mean there isn't a bit of magic to it!

On Solstice, some people dress themselves like Green Men and Women, donning wreaths and clothing made from sticks, leaves, and flowers. On the Latvian Solstice holiday Jāņi, people decorate their homes, their cattle, and even their cars with oak leaves and meadow flowers.

We sometimes decorate ourselves and our belongings with natural patterns and camouflage, but it goes both ways. Can you find examples in your neighborhood of nature taking over the human-made world? Maybe you can find a building covered in ivy. Or perhaps you pass an abandoned lot filled with tall grasses and wildflowers. Keep an eye out, and don't forget to look down— even the sidewalks can be cracked apart by vegetation. Nature will always find a way!

PLANTS & ANIMALS OF THE SEASON

In the Garden

By Midsummer, the seeds we planted in the Spring have hopefully grown big and strong. This is no small feat. It's been a collaboration among you, the plant, and the gifts of nature—sun, water, dirt, air.

According to folklore, herbs harvested on Midsummer's Eve (the night before Summer Solstice) are extra powerful. So go ahead and gather! Use a pair of gardening scissors to snip stems low to the ground. Never take all of a plant; leave some so it can continue to grow!

In the case of chamomile, pop off those little flower heads every other day as they open up. Just as the mythical beast the HYDRA sprouted new heads where others had been severed, the chamomile will grow new blooms in place of those you harvest.

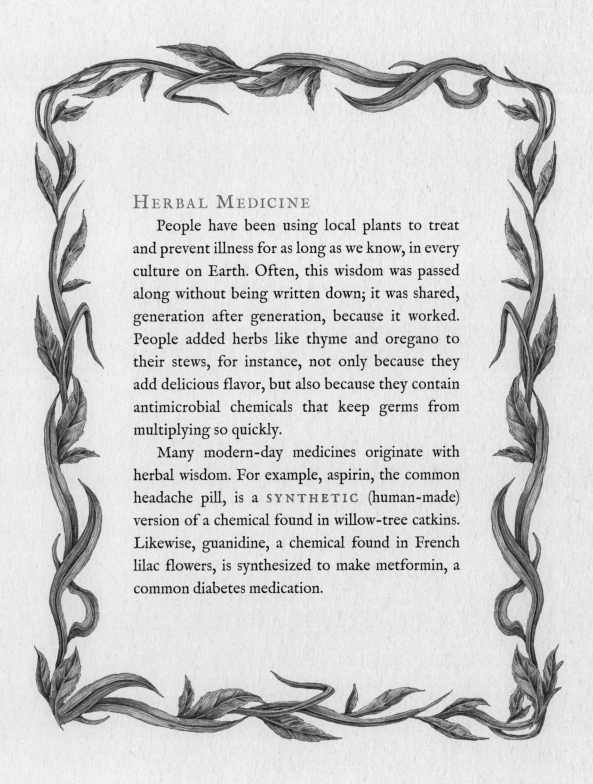

HERBAL MEDICINE

People have been using local plants to treat and prevent illness for as long as we know, in every culture on Earth. Often, this wisdom was passed along without being written down; it was shared, generation after generation, because it worked. People added herbs like thyme and oregano to their stews, for instance, not only because they add delicious flavor, but also because they contain antimicrobial chemicals that keep germs from multiplying so quickly.

Many modern-day medicines originate with herbal wisdom. For example, aspirin, the common headache pill, is a SYNTHETIC (human-made) version of a chemical found in willow-tree catkins. Likewise, guanidine, a chemical found in French lilac flowers, is synthesized to make metformin, a common diabetes medication.

chamomile

BASIC HERBARIUM

rosemary

ROSE (*Rosa*)

❀ calming
❀ soothes the skin
❀ associated with beauty and love

*Both rose petals and rosehips
(the seedpods of the rose plant)
have these properties.*

rose

comfrey

echinacea

oregano

ECHINACEA (*Echinacea*)

OREGANO (*Origanum*)

❀ protects against bacteria, fungus, and viruses
❀ treats stomach-aches and colds

❀ immune booster (helps the body fight illness)
❀ produces a mouth-numbing tingle

COMFREY
(*Symphytum officinale*)
* ❋ speeds up skin healing ❋ treats bruises and sunburns ❋ makes good fertilizer

HOLY BASIL OR TULSI
(*Ocimum sanctum*)
* ❋ ADAPTOGEN (helps bodies adapt to stress)
* ❋ sharpens focus
* ❋ increases energy
* ❋ lifts mood

In India, where this herb originates, Tulsi is known as a goddess of the Earth.

HAWTHORN
(*Crataegus monogyna*)
* ❋ strengthens the heart
* ❋ stimulates circulation
* ❋ supports grief

hawthorn

LAVENDER
(*Lavandula*)
* ❋ relaxing
* ❋ aids sleep
* ❋ calms anxiety
* ❋ treats nausea and headaches
* ❋ lifts mood

MUGWORT
(*Artemisia vulgaris*)
* ❋ enhances dreams
* ❋ protects against bad luck
* ❋ supports INTUITION (inner knowledge; the so-called "gut feeling")

mugwort

CHAMOMILE (*Matricaria chamomilla*)

* soothing
* aids sleep
* treats cramps, anxiety
* helps lower blood sugar
* immune booster

Named for its apple-like scent, chamomile comes from Greek words meaning "earth apple." In Spanish, it's called manzanita—"little apple."

Try washing your face with cooled chamomile tea. With its healing properties, it can soothe and soften the skin and reduce blemishes.

EUCALYPTUS (*Eucalyptus*)

* natural cold remedy
* relaxing
* eases pain

Fill the sink with hot water and a few drops of eucalyptus oil. Put a towel over your head and the sink, and inhale the vapors to clear your sinuses.

GINGER ROOT (*Zingiber officinale*)

* treats nausea and stomachaches
* immune booster
* has a spicy, warming taste

LEMON BALM (*Melissa officinalis*)

* relieves stress
* lifts mood
* improves memory
* has a fresh, lemony scent

Crush lemon balm leaves between your fingers and rub them on your skin to keep mosquitoes away.

MARSHMALLOW (*Althaea officinalis*)

* soothes a sore throat
* treats skin conditions
* immune booster

MINT (*Mentha*)

* cooling
* improves brain function
* has a strong, refreshing flavor
* treats stomachaches
* helps clear congestion

NETTLES (*Urtica dioica*)

* cleanses the blood
* improves stamina
* protects against allergens (substances that cause allergies)

ROSEMARY, (*Rosmarinus officinalis*)

* improves memory
* has a refreshing scent
* stimulates blood circulation
* increases energy
* boosts courage

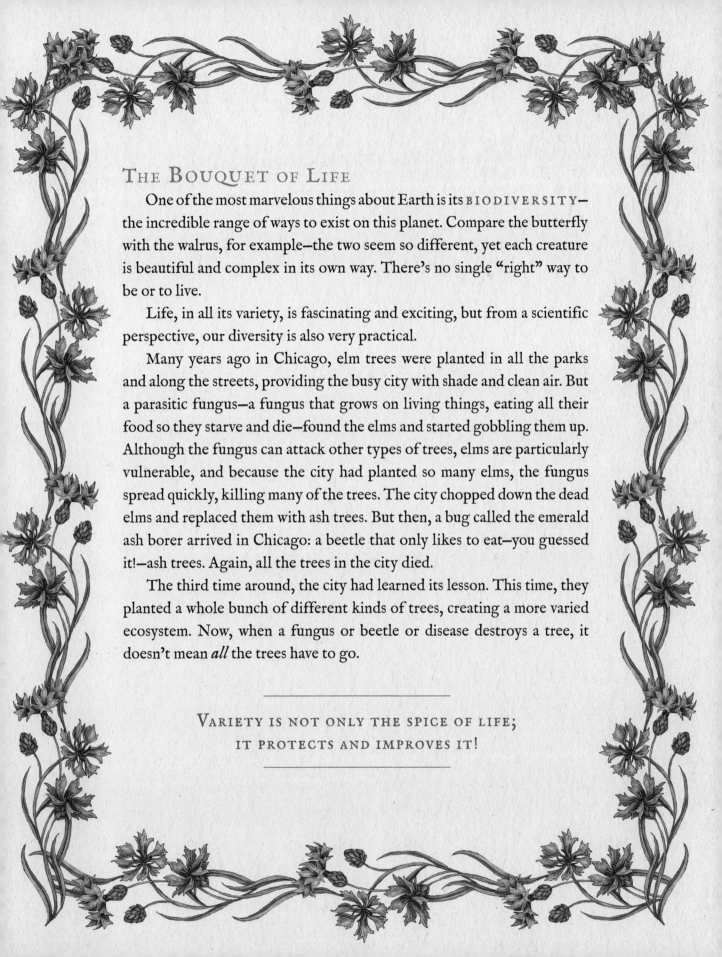

THE BOUQUET OF LIFE

One of the most marvelous things about Earth is its BIODIVERSITY—the incredible range of ways to exist on this planet. Compare the butterfly with the walrus, for example—the two seem so different, yet each creature is beautiful and complex in its own way. There's no single "right" way to be or to live.

Life, in all its variety, is fascinating and exciting, but from a scientific perspective, our diversity is also very practical.

Many years ago in Chicago, elm trees were planted in all the parks and along the streets, providing the busy city with shade and clean air. But a parasitic fungus—a fungus that grows on living things, eating all their food so they starve and die—found the elms and started gobbling them up. Although the fungus can attack other types of trees, elms are particularly vulnerable, and because the city had planted so many elms, the fungus spread quickly, killing many of the trees. The city chopped down the dead elms and replaced them with ash trees. But then, a bug called the emerald ash borer arrived in Chicago: a beetle that only likes to eat—you guessed it!—ash trees. Again, all the trees in the city died.

The third time around, the city had learned its lesson. This time, they planted a whole bunch of different kinds of trees, creating a more varied ecosystem. Now, when a fungus or beetle or disease destroys a tree, it doesn't mean *all* the trees have to go.

VARIETY IS NOT ONLY THE SPICE OF LIFE;
IT PROTECTS AND IMPROVES IT!

The Three Sisters

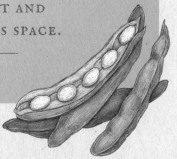

The Iroquois, along with other Native American tribes, practice a method of gardening called COMPANION PLANTING that organizes how crops are planted so they support one another. The Three Sisters—beans, corn, and squash—are a classic example: grown together, these three plants help each other to thrive.

Bean plants, with the help of a bacteria, pull nitrogen from the air, suck it into their leaves, down through their roots, and into the soil.

Guess what corn needs to grow tall and healthy? Nitrogen! Thanks, beans.

Beans are vining plants, which means they need something tall to wrap around and climb up—something to give them structure. Corn grows on tall, sturdy stalks. Perfect!

Finally, squash lies low to the ground, its broad leaves keeping the ground moist and free from weeds.

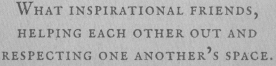

WHAT INSPIRATIONAL FRIENDS,
HELPING EACH OTHER OUT AND
RESPECTING ONE ANOTHER'S SPACE.

IN THE WILD

In Spring, we collected flowers like
dandelions and violets. This turn of the Wheel, you'll
notice fruit growing where flowers have dropped their petals.
Foraging is more than learning what the Earth can give you; it's about
developing a relationship with your surroundings. You can learn how the
plants around you not only change through the seasons but also how they change
year to year.

In Seattle, Washington, there are public orchards, also called food
forests, bearing pears, apples, kiwis, blueberries, and more. In Boston,
Massachusetts, peach, cherry, and apple trees have been planted in public
places to help connect residents with their environment. In Asheville,
North Carolina, the George Washington Carver Edible Park is filled with
more than forty different species of fruit and nut trees, available for the
public to care for and eat from. In Chicago, many boulevards
and public park trails are lined with juneberry and mulberry
trees. Wherever you live, find out what fruit trees or berries
are growing nearby and go exploring.

If all else fails, maybe you can buy some fruit at the
store or a farmers market—but there's something
particularly satisfying about finding a local tree
and eating from it for free!

Refer to pages viii–ix and page 35
(Beltane) for more information
about safe and respectful foraging.

RUTHIE'S JUNEBERRY COBBLER

Makes: one 9-inch pie

Juneberries, or serviceberries, are the fruit of hardy trees that grow throughout North America, but depending on what's growing around you, you can substitute blueberries, strawberries, or blackberries.

For the filling:

* 4 cups juneberries or other berries
* 2 tablespoons sugar
* A pinch of nutmeg
* Zest and juice of 1 lemon
* *Optional:* A splash of vanilla extract

For the crumble:

* Oil for greasing
* 3 cups dry oatmeal or rolled oats
* 1½ cups whole wheat flour
* 1 cup brown sugar
* 1 teaspoons kosher salt
* 10 tablespoons butter, cut into small squares
* *Optional:* A dash of ground cinnamon or ginger

You will also need:

* A medium bowl
* A round baking pan
* A large bowl
* A wooden spoon
* Oven mitts or potholders

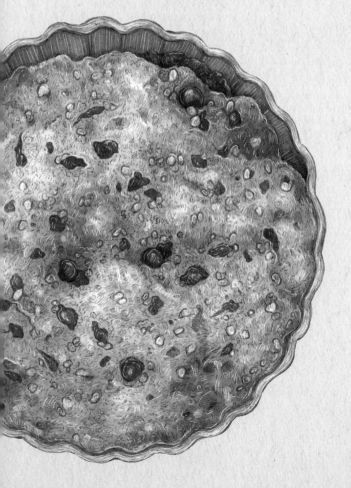

1. Preheat the oven to 375°F. Wash your berries in the sink, pat them dry, and place them in a medium bowl.

2. Add the sugar, nutmeg, lemon juice, and lemon zest to the berries.

3. Grease a baking pan with a bit of oil.

4. In a second, larger bowl, use a wooden spoon to mix the dry oatmeal, whole wheat flour, brown sugar, salt, and butter together until well blended. Spread about 3 cups of the oat crumble along the bottom of the greased baking pan and press it lightly into place, saving about 1 cup for the next step.

5. Spread your berry mixture evenly across the crust, then sprinkle the rest of the crumble on top.

6. With an adult's help, bake in the oven for about 40 minutes. For best results, let your cobbler rest in the refrigerator overnight. The natural pectin in the berries will help it set into a buttery, jammy treat.

What kind of cook are you?

Some people like to follow their intuition and play around in the kitchen, while others prefer to have an exact recipe in front of them. Maybe you want to add a little vanilla extract to your filling, or maybe some other spices like cinnamon and ginger to your crumble. It's up to you!

MONARCHS AND MILKWEEDS

Milkweed plants and monarch butterflies are close friends that count on each other. Before they sprout wings, when they're just caterpillars, monarchs only eat milkweed leaves. As they munch away, the milkweed makes them poisonous to birds that want to eat them. The caterpillar uses the energy from the milkweed to form a chrysalis, and inside this little cave, it undergoes a magical process called METAMORPHOSIS: a complete transformation.

The monarch emerges, unfurling velvety black and orange wings, and soars through the Summer skies. It returns to the milkweed plant, sucking nectar from the flowers, pollinating it so it can form pods full of seeds, disperse, and make more milkweed.

You, too, can be a part of this cycle! When the milkweed reaches the end of its life in the Fall, the plant dries out. Snap off one of those tall stalks, and challenge a friend to battle, using the stalks as swords. Or, if you'd prefer, use them as wands and choreograph a fairy dance! The goal is for the seeds to burst from the pods, so they scatter and disperse. Wherever they land, the cycle will begin again.

When temperatures start to drop, monarch butterflies migrate south, all the way from the northern United States to Mexico. They fly together, clustering close to stay warm, and finally settle in the mountains of Michoacan, where they turn the trees orange with their fluttering wings. They arrive right around Día de los Muertos (see more on page 156), traditionally signaling the corn harvest. When the weather starts to warm up, the monarchs fly north again, the journey spanning multiple generations.

This connection between countries and across borders makes the monarch butterfly a significant symbol to many Mexican-American people.

STINKY TREES

Butterflies' colorful, patterned wings amaze, and some flowers' scents are more enchanting than the most expensive perfumes, but not all members of the pollination club fit our typical image—or odor—of beauty. Believe it or not, some flowers have evolved to smell stinky! Certain trees smell so putrid you might get the urge to run away when you catch a whiff of them. The flowers of the Bradford Pear tree, for example, look pretty, but by most accounts smell like rotten fish. Their awful stench is simply tantalizing to flies, though—who pollinate just as well as any butterfly. Who are we to judge?

SUMMER SOLSTICE ALTAR

Come Midsummer, you may not have reached all your goals, but you've probably made some strides toward them. Today, celebrate and enjoy the rewards of your hard work. Take time to acknowledge any personal accomplishments you've made in the past few months. Stand before your altar and name them. Let yourself feel proud of your success.

Suggested Items: A sunflower, a plate of fruit, an herb bouquet, a water goblet, sun-themed decorations, a drawing or sculpture of a Green Man, music for the ancestors: play your new favorite song, a recording of your ancestors' traditional music, or use your own voice and sing.

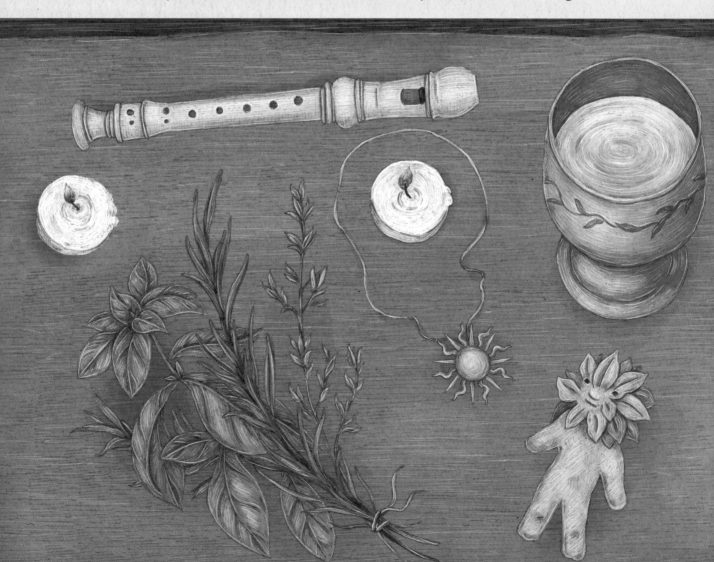

Colors to include: The colors of Summer Solstice are
the colors of the rainbow in their richest hues!

If this year's Solstice is rainy or cold where you are, or if for some other
reason the day doesn't seem to sparkle with that special Summer magic,
try not to be disheartened. Do your best to bring your own sense of light
and merriment to the day however you can. Create the kind of energy you
want to see more of.

MORE RITUALS FOR MIDSUMMER

SPEND AN ENTIRE DAY OUTSIDE!

This is the longest day of the year, so let's see how much of it you can spend outside!

It's best to plan ahead. What will you need to bring with you so you won't get bored, hungry, thirsty, or otherwise uncomfortable? Where is a safe place you can spend the day outside, and who can you go with? What will you do if it starts raining?

You'll probably want to make an exception and have a plan in place for when "nature calls," that is, when you have to use the bathroom. Hopefully your park has a field house with toilets you can use, or you can make a quick trip home.

Suggestions for what to pack in your all-day bag:

The Essentials
* Sunscreen
* A hat
* Food: Try to pack snacks that have protein and not a lot of sugar, as this kind of energy will sustain you longer. Some good options are trail mix, fruit, cheese and crackers, or a PB&J sandwich.
* A water bottle
* A book to read
* A blanket to lie on
* Your journal and a pen or pencil
* Band-Aids or a small first aid kit
* A handkerchief

The Extras
* A harmonica
* Colored pencils, crayons, or paint
* A ball
* A magnifying glass
* Binoculars
* A kite
* A change of socks

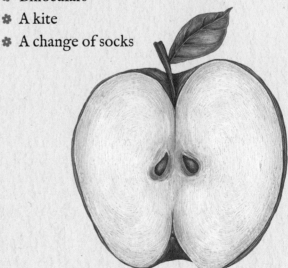

How will you occupy yourself for an entire day outside? Writing letters to friends? Drawing the squirrels? Rereading your favorite book? Watching the faraway birds with binoculars, or looking at dirt close up under a magnifying glass?

Go Deeper: Can you spend the day without a
phone or tablet? Can you convince your grown-
up to join you in sleeping outside, too?

FIRE MAGIC

Ancient people traditionally celebrated Summer Solstice by lighting big fires on top of the highest hills, presumably worshiping the big fire in the sky, the Sun. If you're going to light a fire to celebrate the Solstice, be sure your parent or guardian is present and ready to participate fully. Fire has long been revered because it is so very powerful. It is life-giving, providing people with necessary warmth to survive the cold seasons; and by using it to cook, we kill off harmful bacteria in our food that can make us sick. But fire is also extremely dangerous and can easily get out of control. It's important to respect the power of fire, and that means taking proper safety precautions.

When it comes to building fires, kids can play the valuable role of support. A lot of times in life the main character—the one lighting the fire, in this case—gets the most credit, but no one would be anywhere without support.

Help by gathering kindling, the small, dry sticks and bunched-up newspaper that get a fire started. Ideally, kindling catches onto bigger logs, fueling the flames.

It's essential to find a safe place to build and contain your fire. If you live in an apartment, does your building have a courtyard or a backyard where you can build a firepit? A circle of bricks or rocks ought to do the trick, as long as you have permission. The same is true if you live in a house—ask permission to build a firepit in your yard. Just make sure to build it away from the house and any dry plant matter.

If neither of these are options for you, you can always light a candle on your altar and spend a few moments meditating on the flickering flame. There's something PRIMAL about staring at fire. You can imagine your ancient ancestors, gazing at embers and flames thousands of years ago. Fire is something that has brought our species together for ages.

Double Check: Some cities have rules about how large our firepits can be and what materials we use to build them. And in certain climates where wildfires are a danger, lighting fires outdoors isn't safe at all. Ask your grown-up to check on the rules before you get started!

How to stay safe around a fire:

* Always have a trusted adult paying attention to the fire.
* If you have long hair, keep it tied back.
* Only burn untreated wood.

Untreated wood is any wood that hasn't been stained, painted, or treated with chemicals or oils. Ask your adult to help you identify this type of wood.

* Keep a bucket of water nearby.
* Notice the strength and direction of the wind.
* Never run around or near the fire.
* Don't throw things into the fire.
* Take the fire seriously: respect its power!

Sacred Remains

After your fire has burned down and been completely extinguished, wait for it to cool and dry out all the way. Then, you can poke around. There are a couple hidden treasures lying in the remains.

POTASH

As long as you burned untreated hardwood, the ashes from your fire will make good fertilizer for many plants. Scoop some up with an old cup, and add it to a watering can. Fill the watering can with water, stir with a stick, and water your plants with the mixture for a nutritious boost. Just don't add ash directly to the soil; potash is so strong that it can burn the plants.

CHARCOAL

Dig around and see if you can find any pieces of blackened sticks or logs buried among the ash. Pull them out, and you have homemade pencils! Use the charcoal sticks to draw on the sidewalk or use them in your journal. You may even want to use the charcoal for sacred purposes, like writing down a sigil or intention. The charcoal is what remains of the Solstice light, embodying the spirit of the Sun. As you use it, it will diminish, just like the length of the days to come.

Make Your Own Talisman Bag

A talisman bag is a small cloth bag you can wear or carry, filled with special things that have meaning to you. Think of it as a mini-altar you can take with you wherever you go. It should be small enough to fit in your pocket, but some people prefer to bind it with string or leather cord and wear it as a necklace under their shirt, near their heart. Your talisman bag is something you can grasp and hold in your hand when things get stressful, or when you want to ground yourself. It's a reminder of your own personal power, and the support you have from the world and spirits around you.

You will need:

* About 1 square foot of fabric. (It can come from an old piece of clothing, or you can go to a fabric store or a second-hand store and find cloth in a pattern, material, or color that appeals to you.)
* A permanent marker or fabric paint
* A dinner plate or round lid (in other words, a large circular template to trace)
* Scissors
* Yarn or leather cord (about twice as long as the plate is wide)

1. Trace the plate onto the fabric, then cut it out. If you want to, decorate the fabric with a marker or fabric paint. Maybe draw a sigil (page 102) or other symbols significant to you.

2. Draw twelve dots around the circle, as if you were marking a clock face, about an inch away from the edge. Use the scissors to cut little holes at each mark.

3. Weave the yarn or cord through the holes, under-over-under. When you reach the end, pull tight, and the bag will cinch shut.

What should you put inside your talisman bag?

Include items that have personal meaning to you—the same kinds of things you'd put on your altar, but smaller! You can put things you find on your nature walks into your pouch, reminders of your nonhuman friends, such as:

* An acorn
* A dried flower
* Dried berries
* A feather
* A seedpod
* A special pebble
* A shell
* A pinecone

Other ideas:

* A coin from another country
* A crystal
* A small figurine
* A photo of a loved one

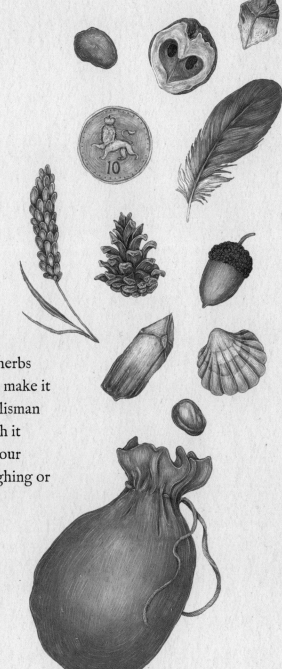

You can fill your talisman bag with herbs like lavender, marjoram, or rosemary to make it smell good. You can also talk to your talisman bag or even sing to it. You can sleep with it under your pillow, use it to wipe away your tears, and hold it tight when you're laughing or feeling especially joyful.

Your talisman bag will no doubt grow to contain some of your personal power the more you carry it around, and when you're feeling like you need a confidence boost, it can lend some of your own magic back to you.

Ritual Bath: Rose Petal Soak

Are there any roses growing nearby? Perhaps if you have a nice neighbor with a rose bush, you could politely ask them for a flower. Maybe there's a bush growing by the gas station, or a wild rose bush in the park. Go on a rose hunt. All you need is one.

You will need:
- A rose in bloom
- 1 can of coconut milk

1. Start preparing a warm bath.

   If you don't have a bathtub, you can fill a large bowl instead, and give yourself a luscious footbath.

2. While the water is running, wash the rose in the sink. Stand over the tub and pull off the petals one by one, dropping them into the rising water, naming one thing you like about yourself for each petal.

3. Pour the coconut milk into the water; it will soften your skin and add sweetness to the rich, velvety luxury of your bath.

4. Lower yourself into the water and feel your own inner and outer beauty. Enjoy yourself as you are; enjoy the moment, being fully immersed in the comfort of the soft, warm water and the lovely smells of the coconut milk and rose petals.

LÚNASA

AUGUST 1

in the Northern Hemisphere

FEBRUARY 1

in the Southern Hemisphere

RHYTHM OF THE WHEEL

In between Summer Solstice and Autumn Equinox, we have another cross-quarter day: the first harvest. Nowadays, many people are less tied to the Earth than they used to be when most folks worked the land to feed themselves and each other. But we can still celebrate the themes of harvest season—cooperation, sharing, and enjoying the rewards of hard work!

The hottest days of the year come in the weeks after the Summer Solstice, as the heat of the fullest Sun is first absorbed into the oceans, then released into the air. The days are shrinking; the full, bushy leaves of Summer start to droop; and wavy heat makes things feel slow, heavy, and quiet, like a thick blanket has settled over the Earth. We make the most of the last days of Summer before we have to go back to school. Slowly, the Sun sets a little earlier each evening.

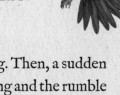

SWEATY AND SULTRY, SENSES DULLED,
THOUGHTS INCOMPLETE . . .
SOME PEOPLE, PLANTS, AND ECOSYSTEMS
THRIVE, BUT OTHERS WILT IN THE HEAT.

The dirt is dry and thirsty, and there's a sense of waiting. Then, a sudden storm might strike, breaking the heat with a flash of lightning and the rumble of thunder, ushering in a cool breeze with the relief of some moisture.

The first harvest is often a time of great prosperity and feasting. But if it's been a drought year, or if some other natural disaster has hit, like pests or major storms, it can mean FAMINE and suffering. Either way, Lúnasa is a time to come together, either to REAP and share bounty, or to lend a hand in times of need. Historically, forces beyond our human control—weather, crops, spirits—were to be praised and thanked, or prayed to and begged for mercy.

SPIRIT OF THE SEASON

During agricultural times, the big harvest meant many hands were needed to work the fields and reap the grain. Unfortunately, unfair systems like FEUDALISM and slavery exploited workers and the land. Under those systems, most people toiled in harsh, exhausting conditions, while a few powerful people took more than their fair share of the harvest and profit.

A good harvest is the reward of hard work, but if people aren't allowed to enjoy the fruits of their labor, if they're taken for granted for too long, eventually they will rise up and fight for what's theirs.

The planet itself is no different. The Earth is a living thing, like you, and for a while now, it's been treated poorly. It's been damaged by pollution and EXPLOITED for resources. As a result, the natural, calm state of balance of our planet has been thrown off, resulting in earthquakes, wildfires, heatwaves, hurricanes, and other disasters.

CLIMATE CHANGE

Climate change, sometimes called "global warming," is the speeding up of Earth's natural cycles. Primarily a result of human activities such as burning FOSSIL FUELS (coal, oil, and natural gas) and DEFORESTATION, it has caused our planet to warm up over time, setting off a chain of destructive events, including mass EXTINCTIONS and other natural disasters. Climate change is not something a single person can fix, but being aware of what's going on, listening, and being RESILIENT through frightening times is valuable. As a child, the most important, impactful thing you can do is have a positive mindset and strengthen your sense of connectedness to your world. It's not your fault the Earth hasn't been taken care of by grown-ups who came before you, but it doesn't mean you should ignore it, either. Do what you can to be mindful, talk about what's going on, and spread the message!

Great things are never accomplished alone, and for everyone to thrive, people must work together and with the land. When we cooperate and share, we double our potential and our options, and our gardens will thrive.

Sirius rises late in the dark, liquid sky
On summer nights, star of stars
Orion's Dog, they call it, brightest
Of all, but an evil portent, bringing heat
And fevers to suffering humanity

—Homer, The Iliad

THE DOG DAYS OF SUMMER

The phrase "the dog days of summer" conjures an image of a dog lying in the shade, panting with its tongue hanging out, too hot to move. It used to be said that dogs went mad in the hottest days of Summer. But the "dog days" don't refer to overheated pups; they're named after Sirius, also known as the Dog Star, which rises around this time of year.

Sirius, the brightest star in the night sky, is the nose of the *Canis Major* (Big Dog) constellation. Historically, when Sirius rose high in the sky, the Greeks knew the hot, dry season was upon them. Discomfort is often associated with the rise of the Dog Days, though of course some people thrive in warm weather.

CELEBRATIONS: PAST & PRESENT

KRONIA

In Ancient Greece, the harvest of grain signaled the start of the festival of Kronos. Kronos was one of the old gods, the father of Zeus, and was often depicted holding a scythe—a tool used for cutting grass or grain. During the festival in his honor, roles were reversed, and enslaved people got to boss around their masters. People didn't have to work, and instead spent their time giving each other presents and playing dice games.

LUGHNASADH

In Ancient Celtic times, Lughnasadh (pronounced *Loo-nah-sah*) was the first of three autumnal harvest festivals. It was named after the Sun god, Lugh (pronounced *Loo*), who heroically defeated the cyclops giant who was forcing the people of Ireland to give most of their food to the greedy king. The victory represented the people's liberation and newfound abundance, as they were free to enjoy the fruits of their own labor. Every year from then on, people gathered to share harvests, cook and feast together, and hold athletic competitions. Another tradition was the trial wedding, where people would bind their hands together in a temporary union that would last a year and a day.

LAMMAS

Lammas, also called Loaf Mass, was an Anglo-Saxon holiday commonly known as the Offering of the First Fruits. In agricultural communities, some people came together to reap the grain in the fields, while others would grind it into flour to be used to make bread. The bread would then be brought to church on Lammas to be blessed, and the people would give thanks and pray for future bounty.

Emancipation Day

Many Caribbean countries celebrate Emancipation Day on August 1 because on this day in 1834, Britain officially ended the slave trade in this part of the world, and enslaved people were freed. The holiday is observed with parades, cookouts, and street celebrations. In Jamaica, people perform reenactments, and the Emancipation Declaration is read aloud in town centers.

Emancipation, or freedom, wasn't something granted simply because it was the right thing to do; it was fought for fiercely. As former enslaved person and freedom fighter Frederick Douglass said in New York on the thirtieth anniversary of emancipation in the West Indies (still years before slavery was ended in the U.S.): "Power concedes nothing without demand." Liberty was harvested after years of persistent organization, labor, and protest. The United States celebrates Emancipation Day, or Juneteenth, on June 19. On that day in 1865, enslaved people were finally freed in Texas—the last state to comply with the Emancipation Proclamation, which had officially outlawed slavery more than two years earlier.

FRIENDSHIP DAY

Friends and bread go together; the word *companion* comes from Latin words meaning "with bread," and breaking bread is a common term for gathering with friends. From start to finish, making bread requires many people to work together, so maybe it's not a surprise that harvest time is a time to celebrate friends, too!

Since 1938, countries around the globe have recognized the first Sunday in August as World Friendship Day. More recently, it's been recognized by the United Nations. What a great idea, to take time to honor the joys of friendship and all it provides: filling our lives with new perspectives, fun, peace, and support! Friendship requires work, but its rewards are priceless.

In India, Malaysia, and Singapore, and some South American countries like Paraguay, it's popular to exchange friendship bracelets on this day, while in other places, people send cards, letters, and texts to show some love to their friends.

HOW WILL YOU CELEBRATE FRIENDSHIP DAY THIS YEAR?

SCAVENGER HUNT

NIGHT WALKING

When the days are hot, the evenings can bring a sense of cool relief. Ask a grown-up to go with you for a stroll around the neighborhood after dark. See if you can find these nighttime treasures:

THE MOON, looming above you. What phase is it in? (See page 187.)

A BAT flapping through the darkness. How are its sound and flight different than a bird's?

A FIREFLY zipping around. What color does it flash?

SIRIUS,
the Dog Star, hanging high..
What other stars can you see?

A MOTH
softly fluttering—
the night butterfly.

Soundscape: The nights can be quite noisy, the frogs, crickets, grasshoppers, and cicadas buzzing, croaking, and chirping in layers of sound as they call out to each other. Can you pick out the different voices in their chorus?

What other
CREATURES
are stirring in the night?

Stars

Many of us know the constellations of stars as they were organized by Greek astronomers hundreds of years ago. But wherever you are on the globe, when you look up on a cloudless night, you'll see stars. Different cultures connected the dots in different ways, and sometimes, their interpretations were remarkably similar.

- The Greeks called the brightest star Sirius after a famous mythical dog.

- In India, Hindu astronomers also saw a dog when they saw that bright star, and called it Svana, the dog of Prince Yudhisthira.

- Meanwhile, all the way across the Atlantic, very far up in the Northern Hemisphere, the Inuit people saw what they called the Flickering, or the Moon Dog.

Same star, different name, different story, but everywhere it appeared, the brightest star announced the turning of the season. How interesting that these cultures, so far apart geographically, all recognized the figure of a dog!

Down in the Southern Hemisphere, the Tharumba people of what is now Australia saw their god Bat with his two wives—Mrs. Brown Snake and Mrs. Black Snake—in that clustering of stars. Bat's rise foretold the coming of colder weather. Babylonian people called the star The Arrow, and the Egyptians saw it as the soul of their Moon goddess. Cultures around the globe have long relied on the stars to tell time, to navigate land and sea, and as a tool for PROPHECY, predicting the future.

When you're out on a night walk, identify some constellations, if you can. Then try changing your perspective: Shake your head, spin in place, or do a somersault before looking up again. Now what shapes do you see? What stories do they tell?

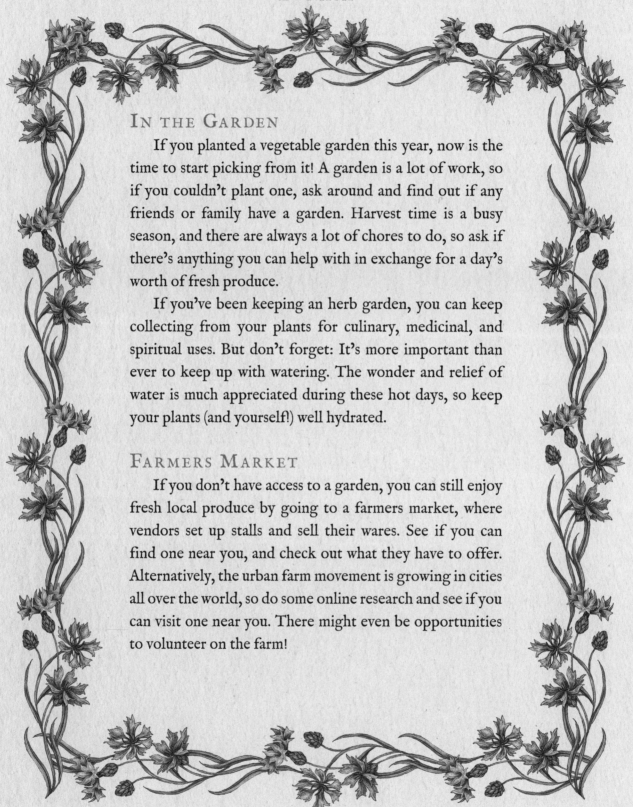

In the Garden

If you planted a vegetable garden this year, now is the time to start picking from it! A garden is a lot of work, so if you couldn't plant one, ask around and find out if any friends or family have a garden. Harvest time is a busy season, and there are always a lot of chores to do, so ask if there's anything you can help with in exchange for a day's worth of fresh produce.

If you've been keeping an herb garden, you can keep collecting from your plants for culinary, medicinal, and spiritual uses. But don't forget: It's more important than ever to keep up with watering. The wonder and relief of water is much appreciated during these hot days, so keep your plants (and yourself!) well hydrated.

Farmers Market

If you don't have access to a garden, you can still enjoy fresh local produce by going to a farmers market, where vendors set up stalls and sell their wares. See if you can find one near you, and check out what they have to offer. Alternatively, the urban farm movement is growing in cities all over the world, so do some online research and see if you can visit one near you. There might even be opportunities to volunteer on the farm!

FAILURE AND RESILIENCE

Of course, not all harvests are bountiful. Not all goals are met and not every wish is granted. But from failure comes knowledge, and often, opportunity. There are almost always lessons to be learned from hardship, though it may take time to see them.

If a plant wilted and gave you no fruit, what can you do differently next year? Maybe it needed more water, more fertilizer. Maybe there was a pest that ate its leaves. Look at the signs you've been given. Are the leaves withered? Are there holes in them? Are they discolored?

This is a lesson to take beyond the garden and into other parts of your life, too. The first and hardest step is acceptance. It doesn't feel good to not get what you want. You might feel disappointed, embarrassed, angry, or something else.

Don't be too hard on yourself. Take the time to feel your feelings, whatever they may be. When you're ready, you can ask for spiritual help and guidance. Even if you're not sure what you believe, it can be helpful to stand before your altar and say something like, *Please help me accept this setback. Please guide me through this.* And then resolve to try again. Sometimes "failures" are our greatest gifts, helping us grow and making us stronger, wiser, more understanding people.

LÚNASA ALTAR

Another name for the first harvest holiday is the Offering of the First Fruits, so make sure you leave something from your garden on the altar—a flower, a piece of fruit, a vegetable—as an offering to the ancestors or a thank-you to the spirits that have helped your success. Leave it overnight, then collect it. If you're keeping a compost bin, then you can add it to yours.

Suggested items:
* An ear of corn
* Your amulet (see page 142)
* Yellow candles
* Bread
* Beeswax

Colors to include: Yellows and golds

Use a sewing needle to carve a sigil (see page 102), draw themes of harvest, or inscribe a wish in the wax

We return to our altars on holidays to reflect on who we are, where we've come from, and where we hope to go. On a spiritual level, we can think about harvest as reaping the rewards of the work we've put into achieving our goals.

It's important to voice gratitude and acknowledge the network of others who helped bring something into being. What allowed you to tend your intentions over the last months? Take some time to stand before your altar and acknowledge the people in your family and community who've helped you thrive. Recognizing the work of your teammates is essential, so dig deep and imagine yourself part of a great big community web. Count as many threads of the web as you can. List them out loud: *Thank you, thank you, thank you!*

Now take time to appreciate the mysterious, unseen forces that have guided and protected you along the way, allowing you to reach your goals.

LASTLY, THANK YOURSELF FOR
DOING THE BEST YOU COULD!

PLANTS & ANIMALS
OF THE SEASON

BEES AND LOCAL HONEY

Bees buzz around all day, collecting nectar from flowers, bringing it home to the hive where they transform it into delicious, liquid gold—honey! We humans have had a relationship with bees since the Stone Age: we provide and tend sturdy, protected places for the bees to build their hives; and in return, the bees share with us tasty, nutritious honey.

Honey naturally prevents bacteria and fungi from growing on it, which is one reason it's been used throughout history to preserve food and treat wounds. Urns of honey have been found in Egyptian tombs, and since it never spoils, that honey is still edible today!

LEMON BALM TINCTURE

Makes: About 8 ounces

A TINCTURE is a form of medicine where herbs are dissolved in liquid, over time, then strained out. In this recipe, we'll be making an OXYMEL tincture, using equal parts vinegar ("oxy," meaning acid) and honey ("mel," the Latin root of honey).

Lemon balm has properties that support your mind and body during stressful situations. For more tincture ideas, refer to the Basic Herbarium on page 62, noting the properties of each plant.

You will need:

* 1 cup fresh lemon balm
* 4 ounces honey
* 4 ounces vinegar

You will also need:

* An 8-ounce glass jar with lid
* A kitchen knife and cutting board
* Small bowl
* Fork
* 2 pieces of cheesecloth
* *Optional*: Tincture bottles with droppers

1. First, thoroughly wash your lemon balm leaves. With an adult's help, coarsely chop them with a kitchen knife or rip them up. Loosely fill your jar with the leaves and set aside.

2. Squeeze or scoop the honey into a small bowl. Add the vinegar. Whisk together with a fork until the mixture is a reddish-gold color.

3. Pour the vinegar-honey mixture over the leaves in your jar.

4. Lay a square of cheesecloth over the top of your jar, then screw the lid on tightly. (The cheesecloth protects the jar lid from getting rusted by the vinegar.) Give the jar a shake, then store it in a cool, dark place, like a cupboard.

5. Check on your jar every day, and shake it up when you do.

6. After one month, unscrew the lid. Place a fresh piece of cheesecloth over the top of a clean cup. Carefully, slowly, pour the contents of the jar into the new cup, straining out all plant material in the process.

7. Transfer the oxymel into tincture bottles if you have them, or rinse the original jar and pour it back in. You'll want to store your oxymel away from direct light, so it will last longer.

8. To try your tincture, add a dropperful of oxymel to 8 ounces of drinking water.

KEEP SOME FOR YOURSELF, AND IN THE
SPIRIT OF OUR GENEROUS EARTH, GIVE SOME
AWAY TO SOMEONE WHO COULD USE IT.

RED CABBAGE INK

Ink can be made from berries, leaves, flowers, rosehips, acorns, coffee grounds, and even vegetable scraps. Beets, for example, make a wonderful fuchsia ink, while red cabbage leaves make a rich blue.

You will need:

* 1 cup red cabbage (refer to page 139 for other colorful ideas!)
* A kitchen knife and cutting board
* A medium saucepan
* Strips of scrap paper
* A sieve
* A medium bowl
* A glass jar with lid
* Peppermint or clove essential oil
* Rubbing alcohol

1. With an adult's help, use a kitchen knife to coarsely chop the cabbage or other plant material. Place it in a saucepan and top with water. Keeping your adult near, use the stove to bring the mixture to a rolling boil.

2. Once boiling, turn the heat down to a simmer. The longer you simmer your material, the more vibrant the color will be.

Tip: Keep an eye on it the entire time. If the water all boils off, you'll burn your ingredients!

steam/quiver   simmer   rolling boil   bubbling over

3. Test the vibrancy of your ink as you go by carefully dipping a strip of paper into the liquid. You may want to keep it simmering for as long as an hour.

4. When you're happy with the ink's color, let it cool, then use a sieve to strain out the boiled material, collecting the liquid in a bowl before transferring it to a glass jar.

5. To preserve your ink for later use, add a few drops of peppermint or clove essential oil and a small splash of rubbing alcohol. Seal your jar with a lid and store at room temperature, away from direct light, and it can last up to a year.

Go Deeper: Try separating your ink into three small jars; add a teaspoon of vinegar to one, a rusty nail to another, and a teaspoon of baking soda to a third. By adding these items, you'll change the acidity of each liquid and possibly its color. Even if you don't do this, you may notice that the oxygen in the air changes your ink's chemical makeup, altering its color or fading it over time: magic!

Make Your Own Feather Quill

Long before there were ballpoint pens, people wrote using feathers dipped in ink. Now you can give it a try.

You will need:

* A big feather: goose or seagull feathers work well, but a crow feather would be really special if you can find one (see page 164)
* Gloves
* Rubbing alcohol
* An X-Acto knife
* A cutting board

1. Go on a hunt for a fallen feather. Bring along a pair of gloves, searching the sidewalk near your home or in the park. When you find one, pop on your gloves and pick it up.

2. Take the feather home and soak or spray it with rubbing alcohol to clean off any bacteria or mites, then wash your hands with soap and water.

3. Strip off some of the barbs at the base so that your feather pen is easier to hold.

4. With an adult's supervision, carefully scrape the bottom tip of the feather with an X-Acto knife, and a white membrane will flake off.

5. Most feathers have a downward curve at the tip. Rotate yours so the longer part of the quill is flat on the cutting board. Cut the tip of the quill at a downward angle. You'll notice there's a little piece of translucent material inside the hollow of the shaft; remove it.

6. Cut across the new tip horizontally. Finally, slice a slit down the middle of the tip.

7. Dip the quill in your ink, and scribe away!

SIGILS

A sigil is a simple but potent spell you can use to gather and direct force into your intentions. The most basic sigil is a name sigil: it can strengthen your personal power with confidence and vitality. Think of it like a secret symbol that represents your energy and helps MANIFEST your wishes into reality. All you need to craft a sigil is something to write on and something to write with.

To manifest something means to wish it into being. Have you ever made a wish as you blew out the candles on your birthday cake? If yes, then you've experimented with manifestation! A sigil, like a cake candle or a fallen eyelash, is simply a tool for inviting dreams to become real.

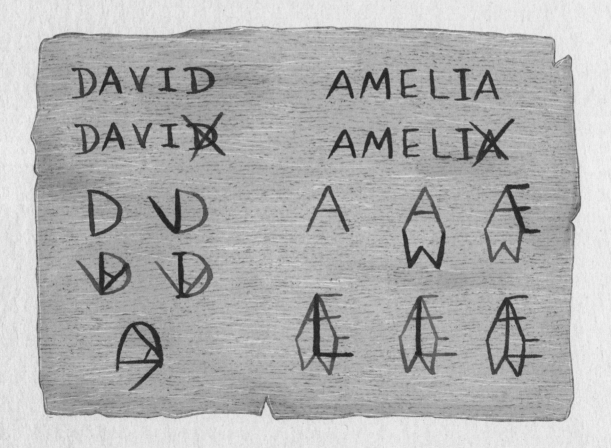

1. Start by writing the letters of your name in all capitals.

2. Cross out any repeated letters.

3. Look at the letters as shapes, or puzzle pieces. You can turn them upside down or backwards. See how the lines can fit together and overlap. Arrange them into a design that appeals to you, that you can remember, and that can't be decoded very easily. The power of the sigil is in condensing your intentions into a personal symbol you can focus on.

4. Once you've designed your sigil, write it on a piece of paper. For extra potency, you can use homemade ink to draw it.

5. Clear any distractions from your mind with a deep breath or two, and gaze at the symbol you've created on the paper. The goal is to burn the image deep into your dreaming mind, charging it with the energy of your desires.

Take It Further: If there are other things or qualities in life that you wish to bring forth, you can repeat the process with those intentions in mind. It works well if you choose a single noun to signify your goal. For example, if you have a big sports event coming up, you could design a victory sigil, or if you have a test you're worried about, make a memory sigil. Sigils don't work alone, however. A sigil gives your intention an extra boost, but you still have to study hard and practice.

TRACING SHADOWS

Drawing without worrying about the outcome puts your brain in a relaxed, meditative state. Some of our best ideas can flutter into our minds when we're relaxed. This reflective exercise can help you access a calm mindset while connecting with native plants around you.

Take your journal to the garden or the park on a bright, sunny day. Find a quiet spot with plenty of wild plant life growing and position yourself so that their shadows fall onto your notebook page. Using a colored pencil or crayon, trace the shadows. Try rotating the notebook, and using a different colored pencil or crayon, trace a new set of shadows so the shapes overlap.

If you're feeling inspired, jot down poetry, observations, or fragments of thought in the overlapping spaces. Think about the significance of shadows, of your movement, and the marks you make in life.

IT MAY NOT FEEL LIKE IT, BUT WE'RE
IN THE DARK SIDE OF THE YEAR NOW;
THE DAYS ARE DIMINISHING.

PRETZEL MAKING

Makes: 10 to 12 pretzels

All holidays are a time to come together with KIN, and there's no better way to celebrate than by sharing food. Pretzels are one of the world's oldest known snack foods, and since they're typically made of wheat— a staple crop around the world—they're a symbol of the harvest.

You will need:
- 1 cup warmed milk
- 4 tablespoons melted butter, divided
- 3 tablespoons brown sugar
- 1½ teaspoons yeast
- 3 cups flour (preferably bread flour)
- 1 cup warm water
- 3 tablespoons baking soda
- Kosher salt

You will also need:
- A medium mixing bowl
- A wooden spoon
- A clean dishcloth
- A large baking sheet
- Parchment paper
- A shallow bowl
- Potholders or oven mitts
- A paper bag (for storage)

1. In a medium mixing bowl, combine the warm milk, half the melted butter, and brown sugar. Add the yeast, then stir with a wooden spoon until it's dissolved.

The word "kin" often means family, but it can describe anyone with whom you share a special connection: those who make you feel good about being you.

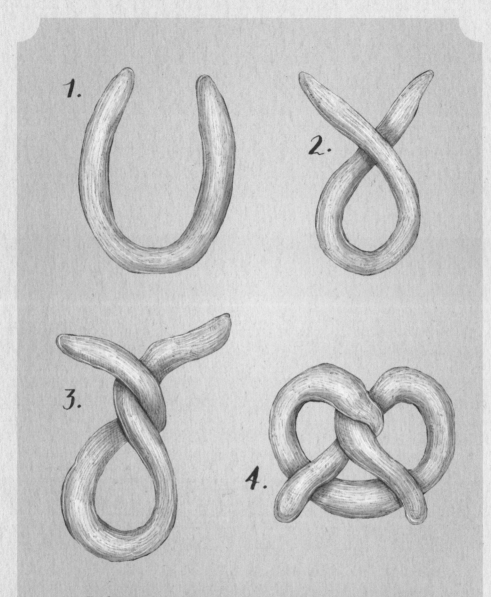

Did You Know: The classic pretzel shape is meant to look like praying hands? Try making this shape with a twist and a little over-under-over. You could also try rolling out three strands of dough and braiding them together, or you could make a person-shaped bread.

2. Slowly add the flour to the wet ingredients, mixing as you go.

3. With clean hands, knead the dough for 5-10 minutes. Press it down with the heels of your hands, roll it, pick it up, rotate it! Massage that dough and have fun.

4. Cover the dough with a clean dishcloth and let it rise for about an hour. It ought to double in size as the tiny yeast creatures eat the starch in the dough and toot out air bubbles!

5. Preheat the oven to 450°F. Line a large baking sheet with parchment paper.

6. Combine the warm water and baking soda in a shallow bowl.

7. Now comes the fun part: shaping the dough! (Tip: If the dough is sticky, dust your hands with flour.)

8. One by one, dip your dough creations into the water and baking soda mixture, then arrange them on the baking sheet.

9. Bake for about 8 minutes, until golden brown.

10. Carefully remove the baking sheet from the oven using potholders or oven mitts. Drizzle the rest of the melted butter over the top of the pretzels, then sprinkle them with big, gritty kosher salt.

ENJOY THE PRETZELS WARM OR STORE
THEM IN A PAPER BAG TO EAT LATER!

RITUAL BATH: A HEALING IMMERSION

Humans have gathered at natural water sources to hold rituals of spiritual significance since the Stone Age. In ancient Greece, each lake, pond, and river was said to be protected by a NAIAD, a water nymph who lived there. In the British Isles and Ireland, people made PILGRIMAGES—sacred journeys—to special streams or springs with hawthorn trees growing at their banks, as hawthorns were believed to possess magical energy. There they would wash any parts of their bodies that were hurt or sick, praying that the ailment would be lifted. They would then hang the rag they used to wash themselves on the sacred hawthorn's branches, leaving it there as a symbol of the illness left behind.

During this hot season, find a natural body of water that's safe to wade in with your grown-up. This could be the ocean, a lake, a stream, a river, or a pond. For safety and comfort, be sure your toes can reach the bottom while your head stays above the water's surface.

Immerse yourself fully, even holding your breath and dipping briefly underwater if you can.

Come to the surface and let the water hold you. It is a precious force. Take time to thank the river, stream, or pond for supporting your body. Give thanks for water in general, for its life-giving properties.

The water is strong enough to hold your pain and can even process and transform it into something useful.

IF THERE'S ANYTHING YOU WANT TO LET GO OF—ESPECIALLY ANY PAIN— VISUALIZE GIVING IT TO THE WATER.

MABON:
Autumn Equinox

BETWEEN SEPTEMBER 21 AND SEPTEMBER 24

in the Northern Hemisphere

BETWEEN MARCH 19 AND MARCH 21

in the Southern Hemisphere

RHYTHM OF THE WHEEL

Mabon, the Autumn Equinox, is the second harvest festival of the year; it's a holiday that celebrates balance, thanksgiving, and generosity. Once again, we stand at a THRESHOLD, but this time when we pass through the doorway, we'll be entering the darker, quieter half of the year.

As the Sun shines directly over the equator again, the day and night are of equal length all over the globe. But from here on out, the two halves of the Earth will be moving in opposite directions. And for the half moving into darkness, there's a briskness to the air. The leaves on the trees turn red, yellow, and orange, then flutter to the ground. Squirrels scurry to gather nuts and store them for safe-keeping, burying them underground or in the hollows of nearby trees. Like the squirrels, we might tuck away some of Summer's fruits, preserving them as jams, chutneys, or pickles that will last us through the winter.

When the days are long, we tend to spend lots of time outside, running around, playing, feeling free and friendly. But as the days start to cool, we spend more time inside. We focus on school and being at home. We hunker down and get cozy.

With this holiday—also known as Harvest Home—the growing season is wrapping up. It's the sunset of the year. Yet, for many children and young adults, the school year is just starting, so this is also a time of new beginnings. This tricksy balance—of opposites being rolled inside one another—is a theme of the season and the great mystery of life.

SPIRIT OF THE SEASON

SEEING BOTH SIDES

At the Equinoxes, there is a balance of light and dark. It's a good time to look at both sides of a problem with the goal of understanding it more deeply, asking why and how.

For most kids, the new school year is in full swing at Mabon, which means you're on a stricter schedule. Summer is over, and you're back to following the rules and routines of the school day.

These rules can be comforting to know your role and what's expected of you. Other times, it might feel limiting or unfair.

Rules are useful for keeping order and balance, protecting people, and predicting outcomes. The universe follows rules: planets travel in predictable orbits; on Earth, what goes up must come down; it takes more effort to create something than it does to destroy it. Similarly, our society requires rules and structure to run smoothly.

Unfortunately, our human-created rules don't always protect or care for everyone equally. Can you think of any rules that protect some people but not others? When you think of the rules in your school, neighborhood, or city, do any of them seem unjust? On the other hand, what rules do you notice working well?

It's okay to question rules. First, try to figure out why they exist, and then ask yourself how they could better serve everybody.

What Goes Around, Comes Around

What you send out into the world often comes back to you, one way or another. The "Rule of Three" states that any energy you release into the world through your actions—positive or negative—will return to you three times. In other words, what you give is what you get. All life is connected, after all!

CELEBRATIONS: PAST & PRESENT

KOKINO MEGALITHIC OBSERVATORY

Way back in the Bronze Age, in the Mediterranean region of what is now Macedonia, an enormous OBSERVATORY—a place for watching the stars and planets—was carved into the highest peaks of the Balkan Mountains. Four stone thrones faced east, toward rocks marked with etchings that were used for tracking the sunrise on the Equinoxes and Solstices. Other markers have since been decoded, tracing the Moon's path, and announcing harvest time.

KALOKOL PILLAR SITE

In PREHISTORIC times, the Cushite people of Kenya created a calendar based on the Moon's cycles and the rising of seven significant constellations. (See page 114 for more about lunar calendars.) Nineteen pointed, rectangular megaliths stand in a circle near Lake Turkana. Each pillar aligns with a major star formation. The site, called Namoratunga—meaning "Stone People" in the Cushite language—is surrounded by a cemetery.

While much is unknown about this monument, it was likely a gathering place for feast and ritual. It was also an observatory, where people could monitor the passage of time and cycles of a year.

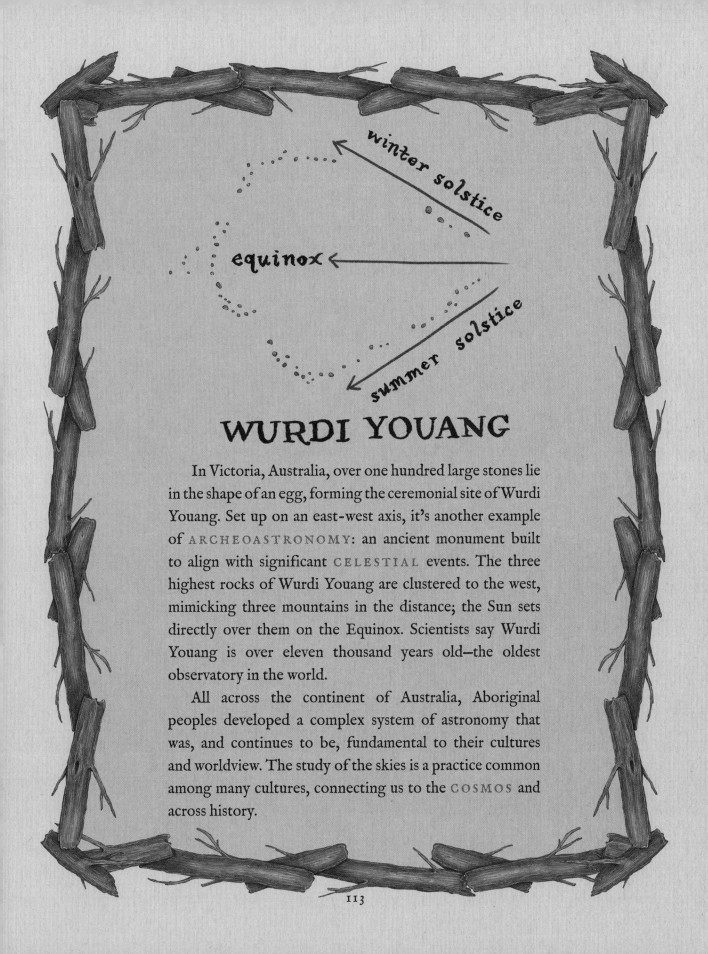

winter solstice

equinox

summer solstice

WURDI YOUANG

In Victoria, Australia, over one hundred large stones lie in the shape of an egg, forming the ceremonial site of Wurdi Youang. Set up on an east-west axis, it's another example of ARCHEOASTRONOMY: an ancient monument built to align with significant CELESTIAL events. The three highest rocks of Wurdi Youang are clustered to the west, mimicking three mountains in the distance; the Sun sets directly over them on the Equinox. Scientists say Wurdi Youang is over eleven thousand years old—the oldest observatory in the world.

All across the continent of Australia, Aboriginal peoples developed a complex system of astronomy that was, and continues to be, fundamental to their cultures and worldview. The study of the skies is a practice common among many cultures, connecting us to the COSMOS and across history.

THE HARVEST MOON

In Asian countries that follow a lunar calendar, the full moon of late Summer/early Autumn is cause for great celebration. It's considered the biggest and most important moon of the year, coinciding with harvest time.

Mid-Autumn Festival

❖ In China, the Mid-Autumn Festival, also known as the Moon Festival, was originally a holiday for honoring Chang'e, the Moon goddess of immortality. Nowadays, families gather, mooncakes are baked and eaten, and people light and carry lanterns. Time is taken to observe and appreciate the beauty of the Moon, a symbol of RENEWAL.

Tết Trung Thu

❖ In Vietnam, the Harvest Moon holiday falls as rice is being gathered from the fields. Children make and wear PAPIER-MÂCHÉ masks and sing traditional songs; in fact, this day is sometimes called the Children's Festival because it's a time to celebrate the wonder and imagination of children. Traditionally, people watched the Moon to make predictions of the year ahead.

Tsukimi

❖ Tsukimi is the Harvest Moon celebration in Japan. People sit outside under the light of the Moon at its fullest, eat dumplings, and write and recite poetry.

Chuseok

❖ In Korea, the harvest festival lasts for three days, and it's one of the most important holidays in South Korea. People visit their ancestral homes and clean the graves of their dead loved ones, then feast, dance, and play games together.

Respectful Curiosity

Every culture has its own traditions and rituals, and sometimes as we explore others' practices, we might want to try them ourselves. It's important to approach this as if you are a guest in someone's home. As a visitor, it's best to be curious but respectful and listen carefully to what the host has to say. You want to learn from and celebrate with the host; not take over. It's the same when you visit someone else's culture. Stay humble, listen well, and give thanks to those who welcome you.

We can admire our connectedness while at the same time celebrating our differences and honoring each person's unique contribution.

PSST — Maybe, if you are welcomed in this way, there's something from your own culture or experience you'd like to share in return! Each of us has something to give.

SCAVENGER HUNT

FAIRY RINGS

Sometimes you'll find a ring of mushrooms in a field; other times you might stumble upon a peculiar circle of grass that's somehow different from the rest—sunken, maybe, or taller and bushier, or maybe a different shade of green. These strange circles look like fairies gathered for a late-night party in the grass, stomping it down in their merriment. And when mushrooms pop up in a ring, they look like tiny tables and chairs. That's why they're called toadstools—stools for small critters to sit on when their feet get tired from dancing!

Beneath most fairy rings are MYCELIUM—underground, web-like networks of fungi. The web spreads out underground in search of more nutrients in the soil, and as it eats, it grows, the circle widening. Mushrooms are the fruit that pop up around the ring as it expands.

THERE'S A WHOLE WORLD UNDERGROUND WE CAN'T SEE—SO, WHO KNOWS? MAYBE FAIRIES LIVE THERE, TOO; THEY'RE JUST VERY, VERY CAREFUL NOT TO BE SEEN.

PLANTS & ANIMALS OF THE SEASON

IN THE GARDEN

Traditionally, and to this day, the Harvest Moon marks the time when farmers and gardeners collect the bulk of their food. Some farms open to the public for apple picking or pumpkin picking during this season. Many towns and cities have fall harvest festivals or fairs with fun family activities. See if there are any in your area you can attend with family or friends.

DRYING HERBS

If you've been keeping an herb garden, you'll notice that your plants aren't growing as much anymore. Preserve your herbs by drying them, so you can continue to enjoy them through the Winter!

You will need:
- A pair of scissors
- String or twine
- Jars with lids

1. Harvest your herbs as you would if you were going to use them right away, cutting low to the base of the plant with sharp, clean scissors.

2. Rinse your herbs thoroughly with water and pat them dry with a clean cloth.

3. Gather the stems together and wrap them in string or twine, tying them into a bundle.

4. Hang the bundle upside down in a cool, dark area where it won't be disturbed. (Closets and pantries work well.)

5. To avoid the growth of mold on your herbs, don't pack too many together. If you have a lot, it's better to divide your supply into a few bunches so they can air out properly.

   Hint: If you live somewhere humid, spread the herbs out on a screen to dry before wrapping them.

6. When the herbs are dry, you can crumple them up and store them in airtight jars.

7. Dried herbs can be made into tea during seasons when fresh herbs aren't as available. They can also be used for cooking, as decorations on your altar, or burned over a sacred fire to create an aromatic INCENSE.

GROUNDING SPRITZ

As you prepare for the colder weather, you'll want to connect with your inner strength. Here's a recipe for an earthy, aromatic spray that can help ground and calm you while cleansing your space.

You will need:

- A sprig of rosemary
- A pinch of sea salt
- A small spray bottle
- Essential oils:
  - Sandalwood or cedar for grounding
  - Cinnamon or lemongrass for alertness
  - Sage or pine for calmness and cleansing
- A sticker label
- Witch hazel (available at most pharmacies

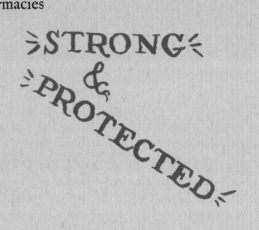

STRONG & PROTECTED

calm AND CONFIDENT.

Add the salt and rosemary to the bottle, then add a dropperful of the oils you've chosen. Fill the rest of the bottle with witch hazel, screw on the lid, and shake until blended. You can stick or tape a label onto your bottle, noting the ingredients and the date.

Tip: Don't spray the spritz directly onto your skin as the oil (especially the cinnamon) might irritate it. Instead, spray it onto your clothes, or around your bedroom or altar. Speak the qualities you wish to summon aloud.

nourishing & generous

Mary the Prophetess was a medieval alchemist from Alexandria, Egypt. ALCHEMY was an ancient, magical precursor to chemistry whereby philosophers would try to transform one substance into another. The most famous alchemical experiments were quests to turn lead into gold and to discover what was called the "universal elixir"—a recipe for eternal life. Mary invented the bain-marie (or a hot-water bath) to melt solids at a constant gentle heat without burning or boiling them. Although she originally used it to transform metals, the bain-marie is still used in cooking, soapmaking, and chemistry to this day. Try using one to make your own balm.

LAVENDER BALM

A balm is a type of medicine you put on your skin to soothe and soften it. Balms provide moisture and encourage the skin to heal. As the days get shorter, the air gets cooler and dryer, which can dry out your skin, too. Lip balms are a common type of balm since the skin on and around the mouth chaps easily, but you can apply balm anywhere your skin feels dry.

In this recipe, we're using lavender to make a nice-smelling, soothing balm, but you can substitute and/or add different herbs, depending on what qualities you want your balm to have. (Refer to the Basic Herbarium on page 62.)

You will need:

- A medium saucepan
- ¼ cup lavender (or herb of your choosing), chopped
- ¼ cup olive oil
- A heat-resistant measuring cup
- A wooden spoon
- A wire mesh tea strainer
- Oven mitt or potholder
- Mug
- ¼ cup beeswax (You can often find beeswax for sale at farmers markets!)
- A few small jars with lids
- Sticker labels

1. First, fill the saucepan with a couple inches of water. With an adult's help, put it on the stove and get the water boiling. Once it's bubbling, turn the heat down to a gentle simmer.

2. While the water is heating up, place the herbs in the heat-resistant measuring cup. Cover them with olive oil.

3. Ask your adult to carefully place the measuring cup into the simmering water so that it rests on the bottom of the pan. Make sure no water seeps into the cup.

4. Let the herb and oil mixture heat up for about 20 minutes. Stir it regularly with the wooden spoon, so the oils from the plants infuse the olive oil.

5. Place the wire mesh strainer over a clean mug.

6. Turn off the stove. Have your adult use an oven mitt or potholder to remove the measuring cup from the simmering water.

7. Strain the plant material out of the oil by pouring the oil through the mesh into your mug.

8. Once you've separated all the plant material from the oil, pour the oil back into the measuring cup, and return the cup to the saucepan. Turn the stove back on and bring the water to a low boil.

9. Add the beeswax to the measuring cup. Keep a close eye on it, stirring continuously, encouraging the wax to melt and mix with the oil. When everything looks smooth and evenly blended, turn off the stove.

10. Pour your potion into jars and wait for it to cool and harden.

11. Label the jars, giving your balm a name! Also list the ingredients you used and today's date. Store your balm at room temperature, and it should last up to a year.

In the Wild

One of Earth's most amazing magic tricks is PHOTOSYNTHESIS: how trees transform light into food. Plant leaves get their green color from a pigment called CHLOROPHYLL, which is basically stored sunlight. (Check out pages 99 and 139 to learn how to extract chlorophyll and other colored pigments to make inks and dyes.) As the days shorten, there's less light for the leaves to eat, so they use what they have stored. The green fades, revealing the colors underneath: red, orange, yellow, gold, and sometimes even purple.

Like us, the Autumn trees are preparing for the colder, darker months. They draw their energy down, storing it in their roots, and shed their leaves.

ginkgo

elm

hawthorn

willow

locust

oak

birch

maple

Autumn Leaf Mobile

A leaf mobile is a beautiful symbol of Mabon. Just as the
Earth is divided equally between light and dark at this time,
a mobile requires careful balance to hang properly.

You will need:
- A lightweight stick
- String or twine of various lengths
- Autumn leaves
- A hammer and nail

1. Gather fallen leaves in a variety of shapes
   and colors. See if you can identify what
   kinds of trees they came from as you
   collect them!

2. Tie a piece of string to each leaf stem.

3. Tie the other end of each string to the stick.

4. Cut a longer piece of string (about twice the length of the stick) and
   tie it to each end of the stick, creating a triangle-shaped hanger.

5. Hang your finished mobile as you would a picture frame, draping the
   hanger over a nail in the wall.

MUSHROOMS

Mushrooms are funny creatures that come in many shapes and sizes. They aren't plants, nor are they animals. They're their own thing—FUNGI!

Keep a look out for mushrooms whenever you go walking. When you come across them, you're actually seeing the fruit of a much bigger organism, most of which sprawls underground: a vast, thready web called mycelium.

Mushrooms get their food in different ways:

Saprotrophic mushrooms eat dead things, so you'll find them growing on fallen logs, where they assist in the process of decay, turning dead wood and leaves into rich dirt as they eat and digest.

Mushrooms coexist with other living things, like trees.

Sometimes a mycorrhizal relationship is parasitic, and the mushroom eats the living thing's nutrients, causing some harm to the host.

Other times, the organisms help each other out, in a process called MUTUALISM. Mushrooms nestle among the roots of living trees, providing the tree with moisture and nutrients while receiving sugars to eat in exchange.

SOME ORCHIDS DIE IF
THEIR MUSHROOM FRIENDS AREN'T
GROWING NEXT TO THEM!

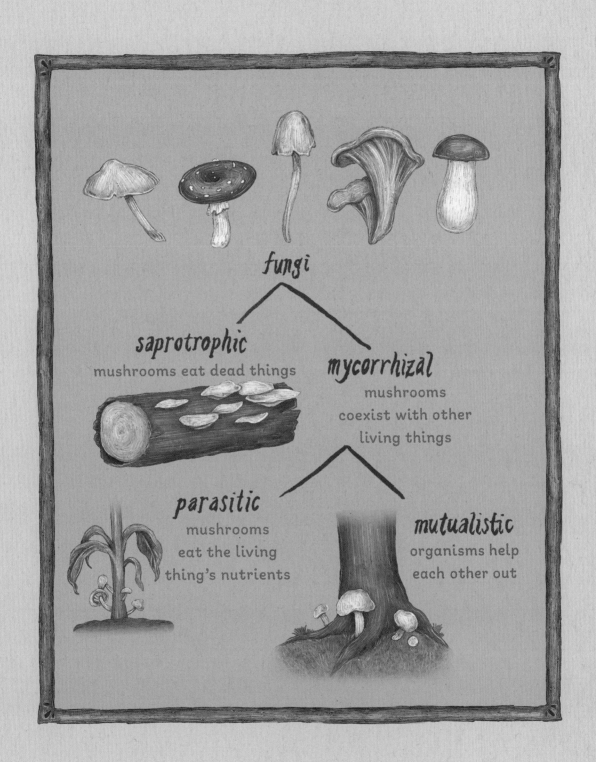

fungi

saprotrophic
mushrooms eat dead things

mycorrhizal
mushrooms
coexist with other
living things

parasitic
mushrooms
eat the living
thing's nutrients

mutualistic
organisms help
each other out

THE WOOD WIDE WEB

Being in a forest or garden brings many people
a sense of peace. At first glance, the plants and trees seem
passive and still, rooted in their spots. But look a little closer, and
you'll realize forests are very busy places, with all kinds of creatures
bustling around. And the forest floor—a world hidden beneath our feet—is an
especially active and complex part of that ecosystem!

Take fungi's mycelium, for example.
The HYPHAE (threads) of the mycelium wrap around roots of different plants and
trees and can transmit messages among them, often
across great distances. This way, plants can
send each other warnings about potential
threats and emit special chemicals
that ward off dangerous pests. This
complex and effective system of
communication is nicknamed
the "internet of the forest"
or "the wood wide web."

But the purpose of the mycelium web isn't to share funny videos and memes. It's to ensure balance within the community, making sure all beings are supported equally. For example, in a forest, the shade of tall trees can block young saplings from getting the sunlight they need to grow bigger. To account for this, the taller, older trees help the new generation by sharing nutrients with them, sending carbon down their trunks and through their roots, feeding the saplings through mycelium. Some plants even share nutrients with different species!

HOW CAN WE MIMIC THE FOREST FLOOR?

Many city neighborhoods form MUTUAL AID groups, where members of a community organize and communicate with one another to make sure everyone is taken care of. Neighbors donate and gather resources like food, clothes, and other supplies, and put together fundraisers to support friends who are struggling. Look online and see if there's a mutual aid network in your area!

AUTUMN EQUINOX ALTAR

Suggested items: Dried Autumn leaves and/or your leaf mobile, a woven basket, an apple, acorns, gourds, a scale to represent balance, stones

Colors to include: Red, yellow, orange, and brown

When you visit your altar during the Autumn Equinox, consider the balance of light and dark with an attitude of acceptance. Keep in mind that while there are some things we can control, others we must accept. Since we have officially entered the darker half of the year, it's useful to spend some time alone with yourself as our focus shifts inward.

There's a rhythm to being alive: your heartbeat, your pulse, your muscles, your lungs, your intestines all contract, release, and repeat. The cycles of life flow like music, with highs and lows. The heart fills with blood, then sends it to circulate throughout the body. The lungs swell with air when you inhale, then empty to exhale. Muscles tighten and relax to allow movement. This pattern of growth and release, of increase followed by decrease, makes the Wheel of the Year turn, too.

Spend some time before your altar just breathing. Take a long inhale while counting to five in your head—*one, two, three, four, five*—hold it—and then slowly, slowly release, taking just as much time, if not longer, to let go.

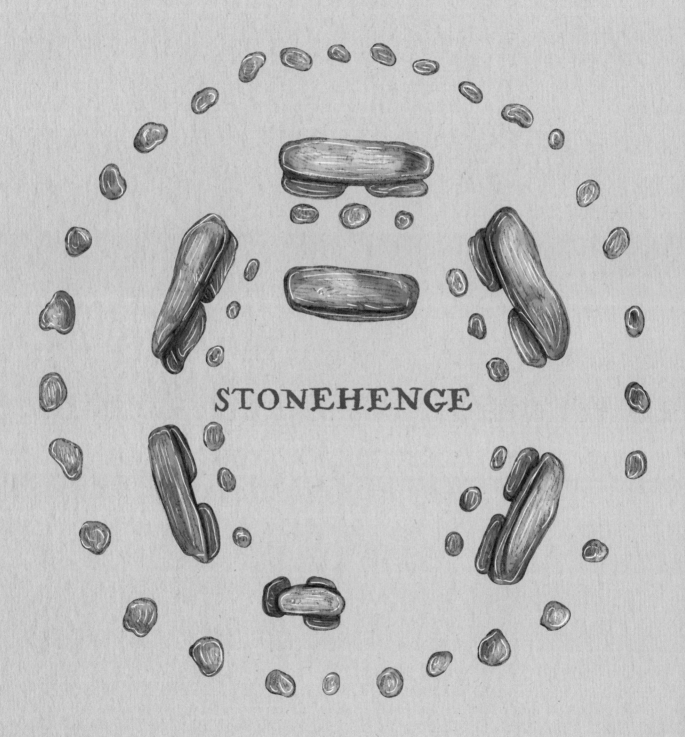

STONEHENGE

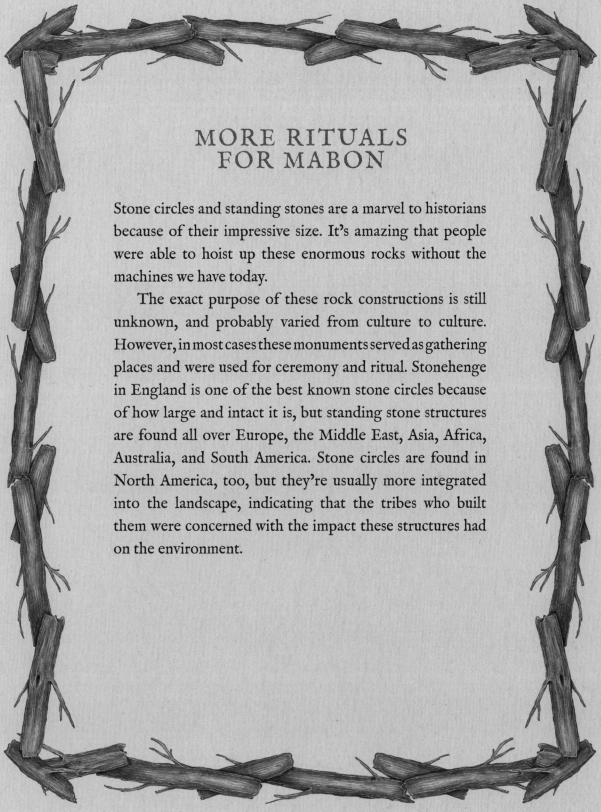

MORE RITUALS
FOR MABON

Stone circles and standing stones are a marvel to historians because of their impressive size. It's amazing that people were able to hoist up these enormous rocks without the machines we have today.

The exact purpose of these rock constructions is still unknown, and probably varied from culture to culture. However, in most cases these monuments served as gathering places and were used for ceremony and ritual. Stonehenge in England is one of the best known stone circles because of how large and intact it is, but standing stone structures are found all over Europe, the Middle East, Asia, Africa, Australia, and South America. Stone circles are found in North America, too, but they're usually more integrated into the landscape, indicating that the tribes who built them were concerned with the impact these structures had on the environment.

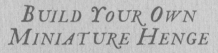

BUILD YOUR OWN MINIATURE HENGE

To get an idea of the balance, patience, and effort it takes to create a stone circle, try your hand at making your own small-scale version.

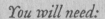

You will need:

* ❋ Several oblong rocks, about the size of your palm
* ❋ *Optional:* A small shovel; a compass

1. Once you've gathered your rocks, find a sandy dirt patch to use as a building site. A true henge has a curved ditch inside the outer ring. Carve a shallow hole into the ground with your hands or a small shovel; it can serve as a guide for where to place your stones.

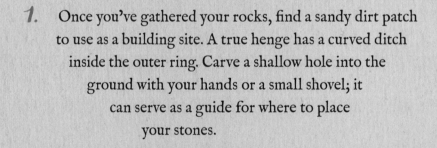

2. Wedge your bigger stones—your megaliths—into the earth, evenly spaced around the outer edge of the ditch.

Note: If you want the Sun to set between two stones, use a compass to find west. Leave a gap so the entrance to your circle faces that direction. To align your entrance with the sunrise, open your circle to the east.

3. Now here comes the tricky part: balancing the lintel stones across the tops of your megaliths to make arches. You can start by constructing a DOLMEN—a table-like structure where two or more upright stones support one large flat one.

Imagine how much harder this would be if each stone weighed as much as an elephant, like the ones at Stonehenge!

Keep in mind that henges aren't always made of stone; remnants of an ancient wood henge were discovered two miles away from famous Stonehenge. There's even a car henge in Nebraska! So, if your stones keep toppling over, get creative, and think of a different material to build with.

Remember: Henges weren't built in a day, or even a lifetime. Most were worked on for generations, as children and grandchildren continued the work their elders had begun.

AUTOMATIC WRITING

We make most decisions with our conscious, thinking mind: we weigh benefits, assess risks, and act based on what we predict the outcome will be. But there's another kind of mind called the SUBCONSCIOUS. This is the creative mind, the dreaming mind, and the source of our intuition—information that comes from deep inside us. Other forms of subconscious information might come from something bigger—what some people call the COLLECTIVE CONSCIOUSNESS, or the knowledge all beings share.

Automatic writing—also called spirit writing or psychography—is a form of writing where the writer isn't consciously aware of what they're writing. Some people think of automatic writing as the hand being guided by a spiritual force; others explain it as a release of what's buried in the subconscious mind. Still others believe it's a way of connecting to the collective consciousness. However you understand it, automatic writing can provide interesting, uncanny results, and has been practiced by writers, artists, and psychologists for generations.

Just as you might exercise your conscious mind by doing logic puzzles or math, it's useful to exercise your subconscious mind. Intuitive exercises like divination (see page 170) can be helpful, as can spirit writing.

Start by grounding yourself. Find a quiet, comfortable space in which to write. With an adult's permission, light a candle. If that's not possible, spray some Grounding Spritz (see page 120) around your workspace, remembering not to spray your skin directly. Set down a sheet of paper or open your journal to a blank page. Place a rock at the top of the paper and set a timer for five minutes. Close your eyes and take three slow, deep breaths in and out. Say aloud, or silently: I am ready and open.

Hit "start" on your timer, pick up your pen, and, without thinking, write whatever comes out! It might not even be letters the first time you try it. Keep your hand moving constantly; don't think about it, don't judge, and don't correct any spelling or grammar errors as you go. If you can, keep your eyes closed, so you're not tempted to reread as you write.

When the timer sounds, put down the pen. If you lit a candle, blow it out. Now take a little break: walk to the kitchen, pour a glass of water, and drink it.

Come back to your paper and read what you've written. Does any of it have significance for you? Don't worry if it doesn't make sense. The meaning might reveal itself to you slowly, over time.

A form of spirit writing was practiced as long ago as the Liu Song dynasty in China (420 CE), where holy mediums acted as vessels for spirits and channeled their messages. Much later, in the 1930s, a group of artists called the Surrealists used automatic writing to free their thinking, creating dreamy, innovative poems, paintings, and collages.

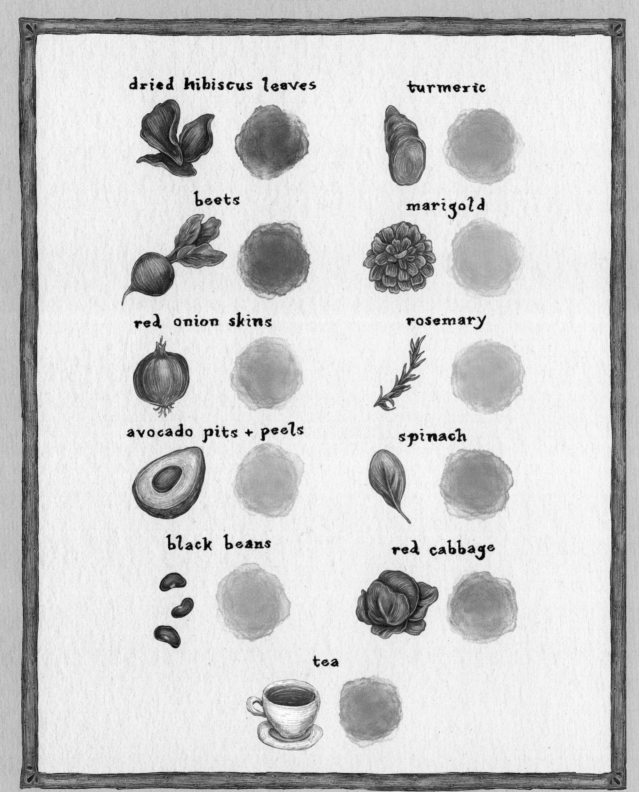

dried hibiscus leaves

turmeric

beets

marigold

red onion skins

rosemary

avocado pits + peels

spinach

black beans

red cabbage

tea

Making Plant Dyes

Just as we made our own inks during Lúnasa, we can dye clothes
with natural pigments from foraged plant material and kitchen
scraps. The process is similar, but the batches are bigger to
allow the fabric to become fully saturated with color.

You will need:

* Two big pots
* 2 teaspoons alum (pickling salt): This can be found in the spice aisle
  of most grocery stores, but it is not the same as table salt, so check the
  label closely. Sometimes, it comes in solid crystal form, in which case,
  you'll have to crush it with a mortar and pestle (see page 236).
* Fabric: An old white T-shirt works well, especially if you have one
  that's gotten dingy or stained. Give it new life!

Hint: The pigments in these dyes stick best to natural
materials, so look for cotton, silk, wool, hemp, or linen.

* Plant material such as beets, red onion skins, avocado peels, and more.
  (Reference the chart page 138 to see what colors are produced by each
  material.)
* A kitchen knife and cutting board
* Sieve
* Wooden spoon
* *Optional:* Vinegar, baking soda

1. Dissolve the alum by adding it to a pot of very hot water.

2. Add your fabric to the pot and let it soak for at least 30 minutes.

3. Keeping your adult near, use a kitchen knife and cutting board to carefully chop your plant material into coarse chunks while the fabric soaks. (The more plant material you use, the more vibrant your results will be!)

4. Place the chunks in another pot, cover them with water, and simmer on the stove for one hour.

5. Remove the pot with the plant material from heat. Let it cool completely, then use a sieve to strain out the vegetable chunks. Transfer the dye back into the pot, or you could stop up your sink and add the dye straight into the basin.

6. Place your prepared fabric into the dye, using a long wooden spoon or stick to submerge it. Once you've given the pot a few stirs, leave the fabric to soak for 2 to 3 hours, or even overnight.

7. Rinse the fabric with cold water and hang it outside or over a tub to air-dry.

Go Deeper: Just as you did with the inks on page 99, you can experiment with the color of your dye by changing its chemical makeup, adding a squeeze of lemon juice or a splash of vinegar to make the bath more acidic, or a spoonful of baking soda or baking powder to make it more alkaline (the opposite of acidic). How do these experiments change the dye's color?

There are many uses for your dyed fabric! You can use it as a cloth for your altar, to make your talisman bag (page 78) or a Bridy doll (page 215). Or, if you dyed an old T-shirt, you can wear it as powerful good-luck armor.

Shrink Yourself!

Imagine being so small that your tiny stone circle loomed above you. Imagine you could use a mushroom as a table or as a ladder to climb a tree.

Take this further by bringing your journal to the park with some pencils or crayons. Find a patch of grass and focus in on it. It works best if there's some variety within your little patch.

Zoom in on it with your eyes only and draw every line and shape you can see. Imagine you're tracing each blade of grass with tiny footsteps, scaling curly stalks, hopping from a ruffled leaf into a tiny flower.

The variety in a six-inch-by-six-inch patch of ground can be incredible. The more time you spend trying to replicate the square on your page, the smaller you'll feel, and the deeper you can go into the landscape.

Afterwards, the world might feel bigger, which means your opportunities for adventure will expand!

MAKE YOUR OWN AMULET

An amulet is a special object you can hold in your hand or carry with you to boost your personal power. It should remind you of your inner strength and lend you confidence when you're feeling shy, scared, or nervous. Amulets come in many forms and are often wearable as jewelry.

You will need:
* A small stone
* A paint marker

1. Find a small stone that fits in your closed fist so that you can feel how strong and solid it is when you give it a squeeze.

2. Using a paint marker, draw your personal sigil on the rock (see page 102).

3. Charge your amulet on your altar for a couple of days, asking the spirits to imbue it with power, strength, and protection. Alternatively, you can place it outside under a Full Moon. Leave it overnight, letting the energy of the Moon power it up!

4. Carry your amulet in your pocket or talisman bag.

Organize a Clothes Swap!

Sort through your closet or dresser. Are there things you no longer wear, that don't fit, or that you just don't like anymore? Don't throw them away . . . trade them in!

Toss your clothes in a bag. Call up some friends and ask them to do the same, setting a time and place for a clothes swap.

Have everyone dump their bags into one giant pile and start picking! Not only are clothes swaps a fun way to freshen up your wardrobe—they're much better for the environment than buying new things. Everyone gets some cool new stuff without having to spend a penny. What you don't need or want, someone else might love.

Bonus: It feels great to wear something
that used to belong to a friend!

RITUAL BATH: ROSEMARY HAIR RINSE

This hair tonic cleans and softens your hair, cutting through grease without stripping the hair's natural oils. The rosemary stimulates hair growth by increasing circulation to your scalp, and it smells delightful. Vinegar is acidic and baking soda is alkaline, so when combined, they neutralize one another, or balance one another out—the spirit of the season!

You will need:

- A sprig or two of fresh rosemary
- 1 cup water
- A saucepan
- 1 tablespoon baking soda
- 1 tablespoon apple cider vinegar
- A fork

1. First, add the rosemary and water to a small saucepan and bring it to a boil. Once boiling, remove the pot from the heat and let it sit while you complete the next steps.

2. Spoon the baking soda into an empty cup, then add the vinegar. The mixture will froth and bubble, like a true witch's brew. Stir with a fork.

3. Once the rosemary water has cooled to room temperature, pour it over the froth. Again, stir with a fork.

4. Take a shower, thoroughly wetting your hair. Pour the rosemary hair tonic over your hair, massaging it into your scalp with your fingertips. Rinse.

While you wash with this herbal rinse, you may want to think about how your own hair is rooted to your scalp—much like the roots of a tree—and how the individual parts of your body, mind, and spirit work together to make a whole person.

SAMHAIN:
All Hallows' Eve

OCTOBER 31/NOVEMBER 1
in the Northern Hemisphere

APRIL 30/MAY 1
in the Southern Hemisphere

RHYTHM OF THE WHEEL

The nights are longer than the days now. The trees' bare branches rattle in the chill Autumn wind, their leaves turning brittle, then fluttering to the ground. As the wind picks up, they spiral and swirl. Fog creeps in, cloaking the Earth in a mysterious, spooky softness. The colors of Summer have faded, but as one season ends, another begins, and in the transition, magic shimmers in the air.

We've spoken before about the liminal times, the slippery in-betweens that defy definition. Things are in the process of actively changing. Boundaries shift, meanings slide.

Halfway between Autumn Equinox and Winter Solstice is a special holiday called Samhain (pronounced *Sah-wen*)—an Irish word meaning "Summer's end." Samhain was the new year to the ancient Celts: a time when the spirits of the past existed among the present.

This is the final harvest, before we enter the darkness of the Winter season. Gardens are put to bed for the year, and the world prepares for sleep.

SPIRIT OF THE SEASON

THINNING OF THE VEIL

---

*"I AM ALL THAT HAS BEEN
AND IS AND SHALL BE, AND NO MORTAL
HAS EVER LIFTED MY MANTLE."*

These words are inscribed in an ancient Egyptian statue of the goddess Isis. A mantle is a thick blanket, and in this case it's a symbol of the separation between the earthly world of the living and the mysterious realm beyond.

According to Celtic tradition, the *Otherworld* is the parallel realm that exists alongside ours. It's the world of fairies, spirits, and ghosts—of peculiar coincidences and magic. Under normal circumstances, we don't usually see what happens in the Otherworld, but there are plenty of stories about people who got swept up into it or visited it accidentally.

At this time of year, it's said that the veil between worlds is thin. Instead of a blanket obscuring the divine and supernatural, the fabric is a looser, more transparent gauze, and we can more easily catch glimpses of what lies beyond. Access to the Otherworld is more available, if we are brave enough—or foolish enough!—to look for it.

EVERYTHING
HAS A SEASON

Flowers bloom, their petals fall, their leaves
and stems dry out. Seeds scatter in the wind, starting the
cycle anew wherever they land.

When a whale dies, its body sinks to the bottom of the ocean
floor. It's so big that it becomes food and home to hundreds of species
for years, hosting an entire ecosystem.

The Sun sets in a fiery blaze, fading into night, then gently rises again
each morning, blossoming into another day. Summer passes into Fall, then
Winter, Spring, and back to Summer.

This is the Wheel of the Year: every stage is sacred and serves a purpose; each
present moment is intimately connected to both past and future.

Change is natural and unavoidable, but when we get used to
something and it comes time to move on, it can be hard. Starting
something new can be exciting, but at the same time, it can
feel scary or sad. It's very possible to have complicated
feelings about change. But our bodies and minds are
powerful enough to hold opposing forces at
the same time. Multiple truths can
exist at once.

HEAVY EMOTION

Everyone experiences loss and sorrow in their lifetime, but it's never easy. Emotional pain can hurt just as much as, or even worse than, a physical injury, and it's hard to share because there isn't a wound to show how bad it is.

No emotion you feel is wrong. You may not have control over what you're feeling, but you do have control over what you do with it. With time, we churn, digest, process, and ultimately, let go.

Allow your feelings to rise, then choose to release them in healthy ways.

Some Ways to Process Heavy Emotions

NAME WHAT YOU'RE FEELING. Write about it in your journal or talk about it with someone you trust.

MAKE ART. Sometimes we can't put our feelings into words. Try drawing, coloring, or working with clay.

BREATHE DEEPLY. Try sitting still and taking three deep breaths. You may be surprised at the relief this brings.

CRY IT OUT. Tears are not a sign of weakness, but a powerful form of release.

LISTEN TO MUSIC. Sing along if you like.

CONNECT WITH AN ANIMAL. Play with your pet, feed the squirrels in the park, or look at pictures of animals in the wild.

DO SOMETHING PHYSICAL. Go for a run, dance freely, or hit a punching bag or pillow.

GRIEF

Grief—what we experience when we lose someone or something we care about—involves many layers of emotion. It can cause feelings of anger, fear, sadness, or hopelessness to surface, but not in an orderly, step-by-step way. We might feel fine one moment, then suddenly awful the next, without knowing why. That can be frustrating or confusing, but it's completely natural.

It can take a long time to recover from a difficult loss. Sometimes, the pain never fully goes away, but we can learn to carry it differently.

As hard as it is, loss reminds us of the preciousness of life. The things we love cannot be replaced. So we honor what we have while it's here with us, taking time to celebrate special moments, people, and occasions. After all, these are the things that give life meaning.

HEART SUPPORT

Just as there are people who can help us by listening and holding our hand through times of sorrow and grief, some plants can support our healing, too.

These plants, and our friends, can't cure or take away our pain, but they can help loosen its control over us.

⬥ ROSEHIPS are the fruit that grow from a rose flower after it's dropped its petals. They contain a high level of vitamin C, which strengthens the immune system, protecting against physical illness. Mind, spirit, and body are connected. If emotional stress goes unaddressed, it's common for a person to get sick. Rosehips can help strengthen your body's response to illness, but it's also known to offer sweet, gentle emotional support.

❖ HAWTHORN trees are so sacred in Ireland that highways have been diverted to avoid cutting them down. They are said to have a strong connection to the fairy realm, so destroying one is bad luck. Carrying a thorn from a hawthorn is said to help move a person through despair. Haws, the fruit from a hawthorn tree, are supportive of the CARDIOVASCULAR SYSTEM—the heart, blood vessels, and blood—and are used to treat high blood pressure and similar conditions.

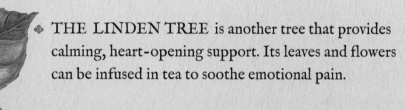

❖ THE LINDEN TREE is another tree that provides calming, heart-opening support. Its leaves and flowers can be infused in tea to soothe emotional pain.

The important thing is to face what is hard, but at the same time, go easy on yourself. Let things take their time. It's a delicate balance to achieve, so be forgiving of yourself.

Remember, a wound can get infected if it's ignored. The same goes for hurt feelings. The pain must be tended and addressed, never neglected. Once it heals, a scar might form, but it tells a story of survival. When your own wounds have healed and you're ready, you can help guide and support others with wisdom and compassion.

ANCESTORS

When bodies die, they decompose, becoming food and providing energy to other organisms in the food web, and contributing to the soil so new life can grow. But what happens to the spirit of a living thing is largely unknown.

Everyone is born from parents. Your parents were born from parents, and their parents before them were, too. This is what is meant by the word *ancestors*. Many people were involved in making you *you*.

Ancestors can be visualized as the roots that hold you up, or as a canopy that surrounds you. Ancestry can be complicated: Sometimes there are people in our family histories we don't agree with. Maybe we're even ashamed of them or angry about something they did or believed in. It's important to remember that, no matter what, you are your own person, making your own decisions in life. Learning your history, whatever it is, can help guide your future.

Not everyone is able to trace their history back very far because some stories have been lost or destroyed. Even when we aren't sure who our ancestors were, we can still imagine them and invoke their presence.

Different cultures have different ways of respecting and venerating the dead; it's yet another tradition shared all over the world. In some cultures, the dead are still considered active participants in the family; they're invited to join in holidays and festivities.

Ancestors are not only the people you descended from. The place where you live holds the spirit and history of all who once lived there. One word for the spirit of a place is GENIUS LOCI, and it's another avenue to explore and respect.

Have conversations with your elders, and ask them to tell you stories about what things were like when they were children. Ask them about their parents and grandparents, too. Someday, you may help pass on these stories to younger generations. *You* will be the elder.

CELEBRATIONS: PAST & PRESENT

SAMHAIN

Samhain (pronounced *Sah-wen*) was the Celtic new year and a time to celebrate the spirits of the dead. The holiday began at sunset, honoring and embracing the power of darkness. Burial tombs were opened, and access to the Otherworld—the world we cannot see—became available for a short time.

Samhain is another fire festival, the flipside of Beltane. Traditionally, bonfires were lit and cattle would return to their Winter pastures on this day. While Beltane revels in the joys of life, Samhain respects the dead and dying. Spirits of the departed were said to return to their family homes on this night, so people would set a place for them at the dinner table and light candles in their windows to guide the dead home.

DZIADY

Also known as Forefathers' Eve, Dziady was a Slavic holiday for the ancestors, celebrated throughout Russia, Ukraine, and Poland on October 31 and again on May 1 (Beltane). During this time, the living would reconnect with those who'd passed on to the realm of the dead. Traditionally, people made feasts and ate them at cemeteries, dropping some food and drink on the ground to share with the spirits. Dziady was a serious occasion, and a precious opportunity to both honor and spend time with departed loved ones. People would make Karaboshka masks of wood or clay in the likenesses of those who had passed. It was also tradition to share food and money with beggars.

HALLOWEEN

Halloween—a night for all things spooky and mysterious—is heavily influenced by Samhain. People commonly celebrate by dressing up in costume and going to parties. Kids wear their costumes and go door-to-door to collect candy. Skeletons, spiders, ghosts, witches, and pumpkins abound as people decorate their houses for the season, readying them for trick-or-treaters.

Go ahead and delight in the thrill of scaring yourself and your friends. There's power in laughter and having fun, and mischief is nigh! But make sure to set aside some time for personal reflection, too, on this special night.

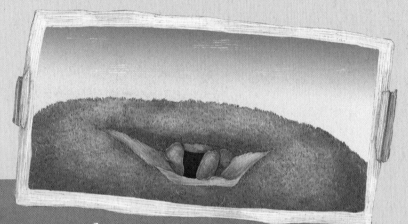

Mound of Hostages

A passage tomb was a form of ancient burial architecture built into the landscape throughout Ireland. These tombs look like grassy hills rising along the horizon, but they were built by ancient people to hold the bones and ashes of the dead. For most of the year, these caves are dark, but on specific days, the Sun pierces through their entryways and shines on carvings etched onto the back walls.

The Mound of Hostages, built over five thousand years ago in what is now the Tara-Skryne Valley in County Meath, Ireland, is one of the few tombs designed to be lit up by the Samhain Sun. Spiral designs representing the Sun, Moon, and stars are illuminated by the sunrise of October 31.

Abu Simbel

In Egypt, near Sudan, the ancient twin temples of Abu Simbel are carved into limestone cliffs. The doors to the temples are surrounded by HIEROGLYPHIC etchings and guarded by four enormous stone statues of the emperor Ramses.

Samhain and Imbolc are similar because they're the same distance away from the Winter Solstice and have the same amount of light in a day. On these two special days in October and February, the Sun creeps into the temples of Abu Simbel, reaching the inner heart, where sit statues of the ancient gods. The gods are bathed in light on these sacred days—all except Ptah, god of the Underworld, who remains eternally shrouded in darkness.

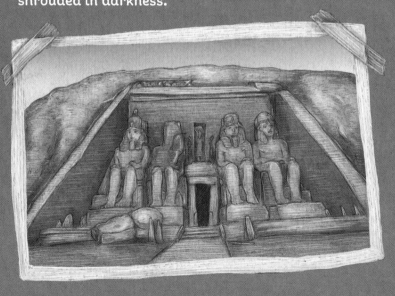

Día de los Muertos

Also called the Day of the Dead or All Souls Day, Día de los Muertos is a holiday celebrated in Mexico and other parts of Latin America, when people remember and honor the dead. *Ofrendas* (home altars) are decorated with photos of loved ones who have died, especially those who have passed in the last year, and offerings are made of the deceased's favorite foods and treats. Sugar skulls, marigolds, and candles adorn many ofrendas, their bright colors a beacon to the spirits. This vibrant holiday isn't as focused on mourning, sorrow, or loss. Instead, it's a celebration of shared memories, love, and life.

SCAVENGER HUNT

SEEKING PERSONAL SIGNS & SYMBOLS

Certain things reoccur in our lives, popping up unexpectedly at the perfect moment. Words, songs, numbers, images, objects, animals, flowers, colors . . .

You don't decide what your personal symbols are; they find you. It's like a secret code between you and the universe. This language of symbols is called SEMIOTICS.

We talked about symbols a little bit in the altar section on page 16, because when an image or object has personal significance, you can support its power by honoring it.

A lot of symbols have universal meanings, so books have been written to help people decipher them. But sometimes, symbols are meaningful to you alone. A dictionary of symbols can help you understand them, but ultimately, it's up to you to get to the bottom of it.

When you discover patterns in your life, like when your personal symbols appear at significant moments, it's called SYCHRONICITY. It can be a fun, magical experience to notice symbols popping up repeatedly, though sometimes it may feel a little weird, too! One way to think about it is that the universe is talking back to you. You are a part of something bigger than yourself, and you are in conversation with it. As you pay attention to such things—writing about them in your journal, talking about them to a friend—you're likely to notice them more often. Noticing signs and symbols is a way of exercising your magic and building a stronger relationship with the universe.

Some common symbols and their meanings:

❀ Bee: business

❀ Bird: freedom

❀ Butterfly: transformation

❀ Clock: time

❀ Clouds: confusion, something hidden

❀ Clover: good luck

❀ Coffin: an ending

❀ Dog: loyalty, friendship

❀ Door: opportunity

❀ Flower: beauty

❀ Heart: love

❀ Honey: sweetness

❀ Lock: a secret

❀ Milk: nourishment

❀ Knife: danger

❀ Sun: illumination, success

❀ Turtle: protection

PSSSt ⟿ There is a whole language of birds dating back to ancient Greece and Rome. The term AUSPICE, meaning "omen" or "sign," comes from the Latin words *avis specere*: bird watching. Birds, with their ability to travel through air and across land, were believed to be messengers of the gods. Some auspices came from analyzing birdsong, while others were determined by their flight. Special bird-watchers were often consulted before important battles. An eagle, for example, was considered a sign from Zeus, king of the gods, that a victory would occur.

As with birds, there is an entire symbolic language of flowers. During the Victorian era in Europe, this language was very popular. People would send elaborate messages to one another using flowers alone. For example, an apple blossom meant "preference," while a zinnia meant "everlasting friendship." Together, they formed the message: "You're my best friend!"

If there's a message you need to hear, the universe will try to get it to you however it can.

Say the symbol of a horse keeps popping up in your dreams. Maybe you see it on TV, and then you spot a picture of one in your textbook at school. What does it mean? Well, that very much depends on you. Have you ever seen a horse in real life? Have you ridden one? When you think of a horse, is it running free, or is it reined in? Your experience of horses is personal, and that's where the real meaning lies. A wild horse running free means something very different from a horse saddled up to compete in a race, and a horse pulling a heavy plow means something else entirely.

To decode your own personal symbols, sit with the idea of the thing that keeps appearing. Write the word in your journal. Make a web, jotting down other words that come to mind branching off from the original word. Close your eyes and visualize it. Draw it. Ask yourself questions about it. Don't get frustrated if you still don't know what your sign means. Often, the answer will reveal itself to you when you least expect it.

PLANTS & ANIMALS OF THE SEASON

IN THE GARDEN

As the colder weather arrives, you'll need to tuck in your garden and put it to sleep for the season. If you've been growing herbs in pots outside, bring them inside before the first frost to protect them from the cold.

Sometimes you can continue to collect from your plants throughout the Winter, but in general, plants have slowed down by this time and won't be growing new leaves, so it's not recommended. You may want to trim off any dry or withered leaves and say good night to your plant. It will need less water during the dark season, but don't forget about it completely, and continue to give it a few sips of water when the soil gets dry.

SEED SAVING

If your herbs went through a complete cycle, flowering and going to seed, collect some of their seeds and store them for next Spring. To do this, snip off the dried flower tops with sharp scissors, then carefully extract the seeds, placing them on a clean surface. You might need to use a sewing needle to open the pods. Careful: herb seeds tend to be very small.

Fold paper into little packets and store your seeds inside. Keep them in a cool, dark place until next Ostara.

HERBAL TEA BLENDS

On a cool Autumn day, you can warm up with a cup of hot tea made from your summer herbs. Combine different kinds and see what blends you most enjoy! Remember: Peppermint soothes a sore throat, lemon balm calms the nerves, and holy basil helps your body adapt to stress. (For more ideas on which herbs to combine, visit the Basic Herbarium on pages 62-64.)

To brew your tea, place one tablespoon of dried leaves in a cloth tea bag or metal tea strainer, drop it in a mug, and fill the mug with hot water. After about five minutes, remove your tea bag or strainer, let the tea cool a bit, and enjoy your first sip!

If you're in the mood for a bit of magic, why not give TASSEOMANCY a try? Tasseomancy is the ancient art of interpreting the patterns made by tea leaves.

Instead of using a bag or strainer to brew your tea, add your herbs directly to a teacup. This works best if the inside of the cup is white and rounded. Pour in the hot water, and let it sit for five minutes. As you slowly sip the tea, do your best to avoid swallowing the leaves. Think about any big questions you've been puzzling over lately.

When you've finished, swirl any remaining liquid around in the cup. Tilt it away from you, and examine the shapes the leaves form against the back. Do you see any images, letters, or numbers? If needed, refer to your personal symbols list, or consult the list of common signs and their meanings on page 159 for insight.

THE ALCHEMY OF SOIL

In medieval times, magicians practiced ALCHEMY: the mysterious process of turning one thing into another—for example, transforming lead into gold. It's not surprising that humans believed in and wanted to control this power, since our planet possesses it naturally. The soil we walk on is a great example of alchemy.

Death is not the absence of life; it's the next turning of the Wheel. When a tree or an animal dies, its body falls to the ground and becomes food. There's a whole class of creatures called DECOMPOSERS, who live off things that have died. As they digest their food, they turn it into nutritious soil that in turn feeds new life. That life then feeds other life, and so on, in an endless cycle.

IN THE WILD
Crows

The songbirds have gone quiet, but across Autumn's gray skies, the crow's *caw* echoes through the chill air. Its dark wings swoop and circle, landing on the skeletal limbs of the bare trees.

Crows are highly intelligent birds that have long interested us humans. In the Winter, they live close together in groups. If one crow dies, the others gather for a funeral, their ritual also serving as an investigation into the bird's death. The idea isn't to lay blame, but to keep the community safe from potential dangers.

Crows can solve complex puzzles, and though they have a sophisticated language of their own, they can also learn to mimic human speech and other sounds. Their association with Halloween and death is probably due to their preference for SCAVENGING. Because they tend to eat from already dead animals, there are many stories about them circling battlefields. This is perhaps why, in many cultures, these mysterious birds are considered messengers to and from the spirit world.

MUGWORT
(*Artemisia vulgaris*)

Mugwort is known as *mater herbarum*—the mother of all herbs. Like a mother, this plant has protective qualities. Some people hang a sprig of mugwort above their front door to keep the home safe. But perhaps what mugwort is best known for is its connection to the dream realm.

Mugwort's tendency to grow in untended, wild areas like abandoned lots, roadsides, train tracks—liminal, in-between places—contributes to its reputation as a bridge between worlds: the waking realm and the sleeping one. With its red stalk, feathery silver leaves, and strong fragrance, it's easy to recognize. Mugwort is said to enhance dreams by making them more vivid and easier to remember. It's also believed to strengthen intuition—the dreamlike ability to know something without knowing how you know it.

Mugwort's scientific name, *Artemisia*, comes from Artemis, the Greek goddess of the Moon. Because of mugwort's strong association with the Moon, the best time to collect this herb is when the Moon is full.

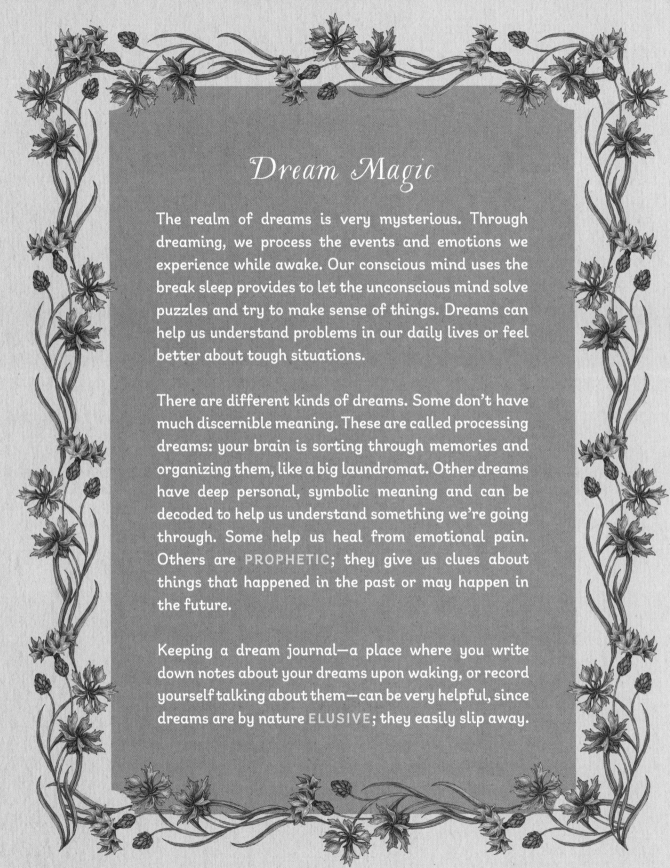

Dream Magic

The realm of dreams is very mysterious. Through dreaming, we process the events and emotions we experience while awake. Our conscious mind uses the break sleep provides to let the unconscious mind solve puzzles and try to make sense of things. Dreams can help us understand problems in our daily lives or feel better about tough situations.

There are different kinds of dreams. Some don't have much discernible meaning. These are called processing dreams: your brain is sorting through memories and organizing them, like a big laundromat. Other dreams have deep personal, symbolic meaning and can be decoded to help us understand something we're going through. Some help us heal from emotional pain. Others are PROPHETIC; they give us clues about things that happened in the past or may happen in the future.

Keeping a dream journal—a place where you write down notes about your dreams upon waking, or record yourself talking about them—can be very helpful, since dreams are by nature ELUSIVE; they easily slip away.

MAKE YOUR OWN DREAM PILLOW

You will need:

* ✿ A patch of fabric, about 12 inches by 12 inches
* ✿ A needle and thread
* ✿ Scissors
* ✿ Dried mugwort and/or lavender, ideally collected under a Full Moon
* ✿ A safety pin
* ✿ *Optional:* Craft or fabric glue

1. Fold the square of fabric in half, and sew along the bottom and open side edges, so you make a rectangular pouch. Tie the thread into a knot at the end and snip off any excess.

Hint: If you don't know how to sew, glue the edges together instead!

2. Stuff the herbs inside the pouch until it's mostly full. Fold over the top and secure it with a safety pin. You can refresh your dream pillow with more herbs each Full Moon.

Just before bedtime, when you start to feel sleepy, make yourself a cup of chamomile or mint tea. As you sip, relax your body and ready it for your transition into the dream realm. If there's a specific question or problem you want guidance on, meditate on the situation while you drink your tea. If you'd prefer to allow the dream world to bring you its own message, you can affirm this by saying: *I am open to the wisdom my dreams have to offer me.*

3. Place your dream pillow on top of your pillow and allow yourself to drift into the world of dreams.

SAMHAIN ALTAR

Suggested items:

- Pumpkins
- Bones, skulls
- Photos of ancestors; objects that belonged to them
- Offerings to the ancestors, including food, drink
- Marigolds
- Bundles of dried herbs
- Incense
- A mirror or bowl of water for scrying (see page 173)

Colors to include: Orange, black, silver, purple, brown

As you stand before your Samhain altar, if you're struggling to say goodbye to someone or something you've lost, take time to feel whatever emotions arise. A grieving ritual can include lighting a candle for the spirit of the person or thing that has left, and wishing them well on their

journey through the next stage. Help them move on, and it will help you move on.

It can be helpful to speak out loud to whoever or whatever you are grieving, as if the object of your loss were right there with you. Keep your amulet or talisman bag close, and light a candle. Say what you want them to hear. Or, if you don't feel like speaking aloud, write your goodbye on a small strip of paper. Feed it to the Earth to decompose, to a fire to disintegrate, to a body of water to dissolve, or to the wind to disappear.

PSSt If you find a bone in your travels and wish to take it home to your altar, make sure it has already been cleaned by nature: it should be white and free from any meat or feather material. Use gloves to pick it up, and wash your hands with soap and water as soon as you get home. When you place the bone on your altar, take a moment to reflect on the life and cycles it represents. Thank the departed creature for its gift.

MORE RITUALS FOR SAMHAIN

DIVINATION

What if there is no such thing as coincidence? The whole universe is connected, after all. This is one of the basic ideas behind DIVINATION, a method of speaking to the universe to receive guidance and insight. Every culture throughout history has had some method of communicating with hidden wisdom. There are many options available for you to experiment with.

It all starts with a question. What, exactly, do you wish to know? Divination works much better if you allow yourself to believe—or at least allow for the possibility—that you're connecting to a wisdom greater than yourself.

Some people like to pull cards and connect the pictures and numbers back to their queries. This is called CARTOMANCY, and the most famous type of card-reading is TAROT. There are all kinds of tarot decks, and the symbolism found in the seventy-eight cards is so rich that it takes study and practice to learn how to read it.

Some people toss coins, some watch the skies, and others throw rocks to receive messages from the beyond. Sometimes messages just come to the person who needs to hear them.

The most important thing is to ground yourself, let yourself be open to receiving insight, and then decode the symbols you are given.

In general, when practicing divination, it's more helpful to seek guidance than to ask for predictions about what's to come. This is because we have tremendous influence over our futures! While many believe that spiritual forces offer promptings or hints, it's up to us to decide what to do.

THE MESSAGES ARE OUT THERE!
YOU NEED ONLY ASK AND LISTEN.

Make Your Own Pendulum

A pendulum is a divination tool that answers yes-or-no questions.

You will need:
* A crystal or small stone
* 6 inches of thin jeweler's wire
* 20 inches of string or yarn

1. Wrap your stone in wire so it's secure, fashioning a little loop at the top. Thread the string or yarn through the wire loop, and presto! You have a pendulum. Now, how to use it?

2. Start by making a connection to your pendulum and getting to know it. Ground yourself so you feel calm. Spray your Grounding Spritz (page 120) and take three deep breaths. Hold your pendulum by the top of the string so the stone dangles.

3. To begin, ask your pendulum a question to which you know the answer is "yes." (Example: "Is my name (your name)?") Hold it still, but as you wait with an open mind, it will eventually start to move. It might swing from left to right; it might spiral clockwise or WIDDERSHINS (a fancy word for counterclockwise!); it might move up and down lengthwise. Then, ask another question to which you know the answer is "no." (Example: "Is my name (a name that isn't yours)?") See how the pendulum moves in response.

4. Keep experimenting like this, and eventually you'll learn your pendulum's simple language. Once you've got it down, you can start asking yes/no questions you *don't* know the answer to!

Scrying

Scrying is another form of divination where people gaze into a dark, reflective surface and wait for a significant image or message to appear. Some people look into water, others a mirror, but perhaps the best-known version of scrying is gazing into a crystal ball.

Find a large, dark bowl, and fill it with water. Set up your ritual space by lighting a candle, and taking three deep breaths. Make sure you're in a space where you won't be disturbed, and keep the lighting dim. Lay a cloth down on a table, placing the bowl at is center. Find a comfortable seat, clear your mind, and stare into the bowl without blinking. If you find your mind wandering, focus on your breath, counting the length of each inhale and exhale.

Don't worry if you don't get a message the first time you try scrying. You can always give it a go another time. If nothing else, scrying can be meditative and relaxing.

GUISING

The Halloween tradition of dressing up in costume and going door-to-door for treats traces back to Samhain celebrations. It was believed that by dressing up as spirits, the disguised people would be protected from them. There is a mysterious power and freedom in wearing a mask and pretending to be someone (or something) else for a night. And it's all the more potent when that mask is one you've made yourself.

MAKE YOUR OWN
PAPIER-MÂCHÉ MASKS

What qualities do you wish to invoke with your mask? You can be anything you want tonight: scary, spooky, beautiful, mystical, gross . . .

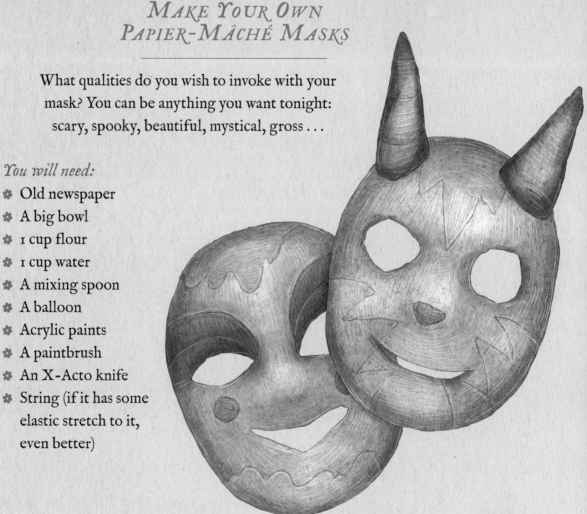

You will need:
* Old newspaper
* A big bowl
* 1 cup flour
* 1 cup water
* A mixing spoon
* A balloon
* Acrylic paints
* A paintbrush
* An X-Acto knife
* String (if it has some elastic stretch to it, even better)

1. Rip the newspaper into strips. Then, blow up a balloon so it's about the size of your head.

2. Pour the flour into the bowl. Slowly add water, stirring as you do, until you have a soupy mixture.

3. Dip strips of newspaper into the flour-water mixture. Lay them across the balloon until it's completely covered. The more layers of newspaper you add, the sturdier your mask will be. (You can use strips of papier-mâché to build up your mask, sculpting features like a nose, horns, eyebrows, lips, etc.)

4. Once you've shaped your mask to your satisfaction, dip a large paint brush into the mixture and coat the mask with a final layer of goo.

5. Put your mask somewhere safe to dry for a few days. When it has thoroughly hardened, use a pencil to mark where you want to make eyeholes. With an adult's help, use an X-Acto knife to cut along your pencil lines (adding a mouth hole and nostrils, too, if you like).

6. If you want to wear your mask instead of hold it up, you can poke holes one inch from the edges where your ears would be. Tie one end of a long piece of string to one of the holes. Press the mask to your face while stretching the string around the back of your head. When you find a comfortable fit, tie the other end of the string to the opposite hole and snip off any extra.

7. Finally, give your mask a coat of white acrylic paint. When it is done drying, go ahead and paint your mask whatever colors you like!

Cultural Appropriation

As recently as 1978, the United States government outlawed many Native American spiritual practices, including smudging. While these unfair laws are no longer in effect, they have left a harmful legacy.

In recent years, many people outside Native American communities have become interested in smudging. This has created a strong demand for white sage, leading companies to harvest and sell it, profiting off the spiritual practices Native Americans were once denied. Some of these companies have taken so much white sage that there's not enough left for Native people to use in the proper way.

Claiming ownership of, and especially exploiting—making money from—a culture to which you don't belong is called cultural appropriation, and it is something to avoid. Not only is it disrespectful, but it can interfere with others' access to their own customs.

By being aware of this history and using plants responsibly, you can help to curb this form of injustice.

Ritual Bath: Smoke Cleansing

The practice of burning white sage, called SMUDGING, is a spiritual custom of western Native American tribes like the Lakota and the Chumash. While smudging with white sage is a sacred practice specific to those tribes, burning herb bundles and using smoke to cleanse is something many cultures have practiced throughout history. In medieval times in Europe, people burned thyme and rosemary to create an aromatic smoke that deterred pests.

You can share in this practice yourself, ideally using plants that grow plentifully in your area. Mugwort and juniper are good plants to use if they grow where you live, but look around and research what's native to your area. Mint, for example, spreads rapidly and is very fragrant. This is a more respectful and sustainable practice than purchasing herbs to burn. Even better: Gather herbs you've tended yourself to form your bundle!

You will need:
- Dried herbs
- Scissors
- Twine
- A ceramic or otherwise heat-safe bowl
- Matches or a stick lighter
- Small bowl filled with water

1. Cut the herbs into approximately 6-inch lengths. Wrap twine around the leaves, making sure they're tightly bundled. If the herbs are too loose, your smoke wand will burn too quickly and shoot off dangerous embers. Tie the twine in a secure knot and snip off the loose ends.

2. Have your adult light the end of your bundle. When a flame forms, blow it out so that the bundle smolders, producing smoke.

Take Care: Make sure you have a small bowl of water close at hand, and be sure to review the fire safety tips on page 76.

3. Together with your adult, use the bundle to clear any stale or negative energy from your home by making gentle circular motions as you slowly pass through each room. Pay special attention to the corners of rooms. Imagine yourself waking up and clearing out any heavy energy that's settled over your environment.

4. Once you've completed your smoke cleanse, make sure to properly extinguish your bundle in the bowl of water.

YULE:
Winter Solstice

DECEMBER 21

in the Northern Hemisphere

JUNE 21

in the Southern Hemisphere

RHYTHM OF THE WHEEL

On the Winter Solstice, the tilt of the Earth is angled farthest from the Sun, causing the shortest day of the year and the longest night. Near the North and South Poles, the longest night seems endless; the Sun stays below the horizon for weeks before and after the Solstice.

The ground is hard and frozen, and the world outside is asleep. In many places, the land is blanketed in snow. The trees are bare, and without light, few plants grow. All is quiet. Many animals have either left for warmer climates or entered a state of HIBERNATION, huddled inside somewhere, living off whatever food has been saved, or the reserves their bodies have stored.

During difficult times, there's less rejoicing and more prayer. When warmth and light are scarce, people must make or find their own. And so, we join together through hardship, creating the glow of fellowship. Despite the harshness of the season, this time of year is associated with merriment and goodwill as we struggle to survive another Winter together.

Even though the dark season will last long after the Winter Solstice, the shortest day is tinged with hope, because the Sun has declared its return, and it can only get brighter from here on. But Winter isn't just about yearning for the light of Spring. It reminds us to find our joy wherever we can. There is hope and relief to be shared even on the darkest day, especially when we can come together with loved ones.

SPIRIT OF THE SEASON

When you're in it, Winter can feel like it might last forever. We mammals may not turn sunlight into food as plants do, but most people do rely on the Sun's light to lift their mood and give them energy. Before there were clocks, people rose with the Sun and went to bed when it got dark. It makes sense that as the days shorten, our energy levels might decrease.

Bears hibernate in caves; frogs and fish swim to deeper levels of the pond where it doesn't freeze; birds migrate to their Summer homes. We humans mostly go about our daily business. If anything, we might be even busier than usual, what with schoolwork and rushing around preparing for the Winter holidays.

Waking up day after day to darkness and gray skies can be depressing. Do the things you know keep you strong, happy, and healthy, and practice them even if you've lost the excitement for them. Making to-do lists can be a useful trick for staying on top of the things you need to do. Put the simple things you take for granted at the top of the list and cross them off as you go. Tasks like "get out of bed," "remember my dream," and "go for a walk" might seem small, but they are everyday accomplishments.

Find ways to sneak magic and creativity into your day, too. Add tasks to your to-do list such as "write a poem," "sing a song to my cat," or "practice divination." These simple things can help remind you who you are and what you're capable of. Try sharing your magic with others who might be having a hard time. Send your poem to a friend or perform a song for the family. Winter is an important time to spread our joy, passing it on so all can benefit.

MAKING GIFTS AND WRITING LETTERS

LOVE is a mysterious thing that probably means
something different to everyone. One definition of
love is noticing and appreciating the peculiarities
of a person, place, or thing that make them special.

During this quiet, cold time of the year, it can be warming to remember the things we love, naming them and sharing them to show our gratitude.

Creating tokens of good will and delivering them to those you love is a good way to connect during this season. It's a reminder that even in darkness, we have an unlimited supply of love in our hearts. (And remember that the love and good wishes you share will, more often than not, be returned to you.)

So, send out some messages! Grab a pen and paper and write an old-fashioned letter, drawing pictures in the margins. Make a homemade gift, wrap it, and leave it on a friend's doorstep. Send a friendly text to someone you appreciate. 'Tis the season!

CAULDRON

A cauldron is a large pot or kettle that can withstand great heat; it hangs directly over a fire to cook food. A powerful symbol in many cultures, the cauldron represents community, as people had to come together to build the fire and add to the pot. In Winter months, the warmth and contributions of the group were especially needed so that no one went hungry.

Yule was a midwinter festival held by the Germanic tribes of Europe. At the darkest and coldest time of year, meat was cooked in a cauldron, sacrifices were made to the gods, and toasts were given to the new year ahead.

Our own bodies can be thought of as cauldrons, holding experiences, processing them, and transforming them into nourishment. Some things are harder to break down, requiring more heat and time before they're ready to digest.

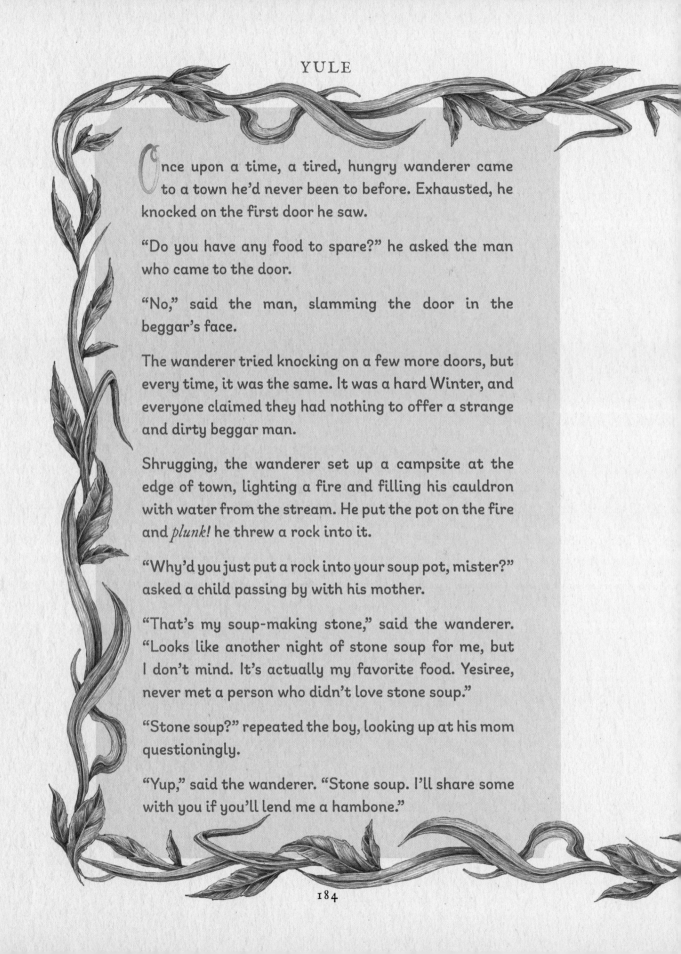

Once upon a time, a tired, hungry wanderer came to a town he'd never been to before. Exhausted, he knocked on the first door he saw.

"Do you have any food to spare?" he asked the man who came to the door.

"No," said the man, slamming the door in the beggar's face.

The wanderer tried knocking on a few more doors, but every time, it was the same. It was a hard Winter, and everyone claimed they had nothing to offer a strange and dirty beggar man.

Shrugging, the wanderer set up a campsite at the edge of town, lighting a fire and filling his cauldron with water from the stream. He put the pot on the fire and *plunk!* he threw a rock into it.

"Why'd you just put a rock into your soup pot, mister?" asked a child passing by with his mother.

"That's my soup-making stone," said the wanderer. "Looks like another night of stone soup for me, but I don't mind. It's actually my favorite food. Yesiree, never met a person who didn't love stone soup."

"Stone soup?" repeated the boy, looking up at his mom questioningly.

"Yup," said the wanderer. "Stone soup. I'll share some with you if you'll lend me a hambone."

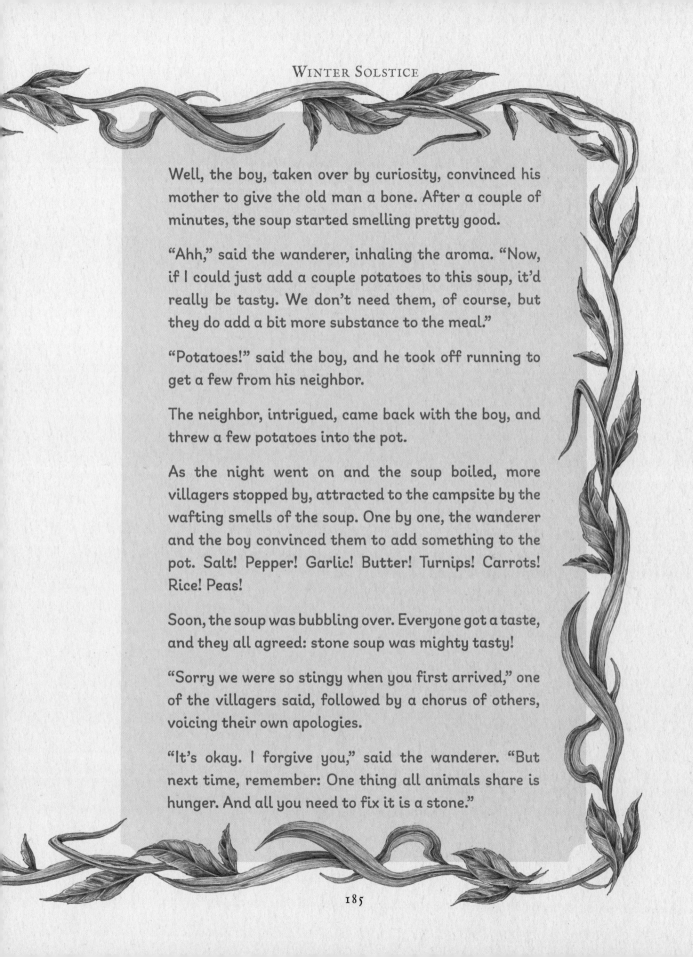

Well, the boy, taken over by curiosity, convinced his mother to give the old man a bone. After a couple of minutes, the soup started smelling pretty good.

"Ahh," said the wanderer, inhaling the aroma. "Now, if I could just add a couple potatoes to this soup, it'd really be tasty. We don't need them, of course, but they do add a bit more substance to the meal."

"Potatoes!" said the boy, and he took off running to get a few from his neighbor.

The neighbor, intrigued, came back with the boy, and threw a few potatoes into the pot.

As the night went on and the soup boiled, more villagers stopped by, attracted to the campsite by the wafting smells of the soup. One by one, the wanderer and the boy convinced them to add something to the pot. Salt! Pepper! Garlic! Butter! Turnips! Carrots! Rice! Peas!

Soon, the soup was bubbling over. Everyone got a taste, and they all agreed: stone soup was mighty tasty!

"Sorry we were so stingy when you first arrived," one of the villagers said, followed by a chorus of others, voicing their own apologies.

"It's okay. I forgive you," said the wanderer. "But next time, remember: One thing all animals share is hunger. And all you need to fix it is a stone."

STONE SOUP

Stews and soups are hearty and can feed many. More ingredients can be thrown in as they arrive, and the whole thing can be left alone to soften and soak up flavor. The tale of "Stone Soup" (sometimes called "Axe Soup" or "Nail Soup") has been told and retold through the years. A familiar folktale in many cultures, it speaks to the importance of sharing, especially during times of struggle.

YOU, TOO, CAN MAKE STONE SOUP!

Potlucks—parties where everyone makes and brings a dish—make magnificent Yuletide feasts. It's not just the food that fills and nourishes us. When we gather together with others, it stokes our inner warmth.

To throw a "Stone Soup" potluck, ask everyone to bring one ingredient. It can be anything! Whatever is on hand: an onion, beans, noodles, a hambone, or some dried herbs for flavoring. Everything must go in, no matter how the flavors might clash. Oh, yes—and don't forget the stone! Part of the fun of stone soup is the mystery of it. Every pot is one of a kind.

Fill your soup pot with water. With an adult's help, bring it to a boil and add the ingredients as they arrive.

Once the soup has been boiling for about ten minutes, turn the heat down to a simmer. Cover your pot with a lid, giving the soup a good stir every so often. When the ingredients are soft and any meats and/or beans are thoroughly cooked, have an adult carefully remove the pot from the heat. Serve with bread or top it with cheese, depending on what's available. Then eat, eat, eat, until everyone's belly is full!

PHASES OF THE MOON

The Summer Solstice corresponds to high noon in the Wheel of the Year, and Winter Solstice—the spoke directly across the Wheel—is associated with midnight and the Moon.

Our year is based on the Earth's trip around the Sun. But older calendars base a year around the phases of the Moon. Many Asian, Islamic, and Jewish cultures use a LUNAR calendar to determine when holidays are celebrated.

Just as the Earth orbits the Sun, the Moon orbits the Earth, its trip taking twenty-eight days. The Moon doesn't make any light of its own; it's like a giant mirror, reflecting the Sun's light back to us. As it travels, the Moon looks different depending on how the light strikes it. These different stages are called the phases of the Moon.

LIGHT ON THE
right
THE MOON IS GETTING
bright.

When the Earth is directly between the Moon and the Sun, the Moon is said to be Full. It shines big, round, and usually white. As it continues its course around us, its light wanes, or decreases, causing it to look smaller and thinner. It passes through its waning phases: Gibbous Moon (where a little slice is taken out); Third Quarter Moon (where it looks like it's been cut in half); and finally Crescent Moon (where all you can see is a bright sliver—like a fingernail!). When we can't see the Moon at all, it's called a New Moon, or Dark Moon. But as the light increases, the Moon waxes back to Full again, going through each of its waning phases, but in reverse—growing instead of shrinking.

MOON AFFIRMATIONS

The Moon was traditionally a guide for farmers. Its phases indicated appropriate times for seeding, tending, and harvesting. You, too, can make plans according to the Moon, harnessing its influence.

Working with the Moon can help you connect to the flow and patterns of life. As you do, it will start to become second nature. Without realizing, you might find yourself getting your hair cut on a waning Moon, for instance, or you might hand in a big assignment on the Full Moon.

These are not coincidences: you're tapping into your natural power! Always make note of these special occurences—and celebrate them.

To become more attuned to the Moon and its influence, try out the AFFIRMATIONS—encouraging statements—on the next page for each of its phases. You can speak them aloud, write them down, or simply think them to yourself as you gaze at the Moon.

- ❧ NEW MOON: Embrace the darkness. Reflect in your journal. Sleep. State intentions. Light candles.

- ❧ WAXING CRESCENT: A time of increase. Plant seeds. Voice your needs.

- ❧ FIRST QUARTER MOON: The Equinox of the Moon cycle, halfway between New and Full. Tend your goals. Consider balance.

- ❧ WAXING GIBBOUS: Nearing culmination. Prepare for Fullness. Build your strength.

- ❧ FULL MOON: The Moon is its largest and brightest. Manifest your dreams. Trust your instincts. Harvest, eat, and enjoy.

- ❧ WANING GIBBOUS: Beginning to shed. Cut back. Give things away.

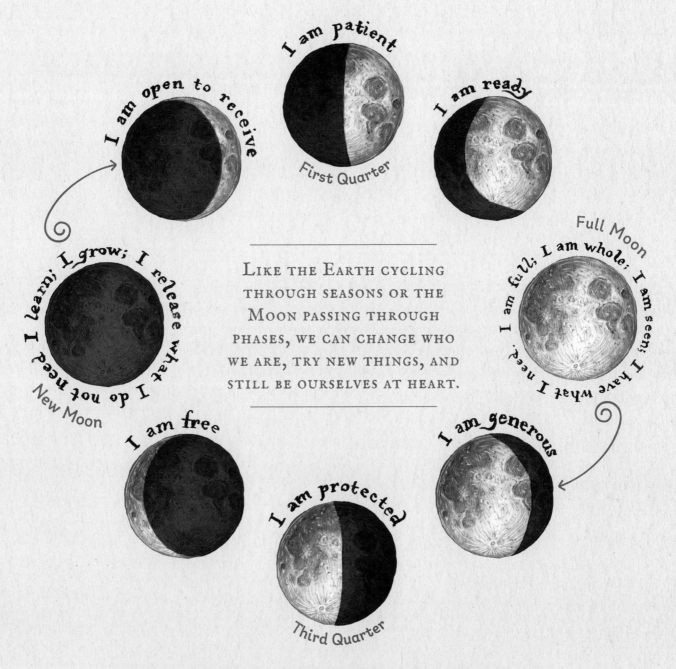

I am patient

I am open to receive

I am ready

First Quarter

Full Moon

I learn; I grow; I release what I do not need

I am full; I am whole; I am seen; I have what I need

LIKE THE EARTH CYCLING THROUGH SEASONS OR THE MOON PASSING THROUGH PHASES, WE CAN CHANGE WHO WE ARE, TRY NEW THINGS, AND STILL BE OURSELVES AT HEART.

New Moon

I am free

I am generous

I am protected

Third Quarter

◆ THIRD QUARTER MOON: Another Equinox, halfway between Full and New. Organize your belongings. Make room.

◆ WANING CRESCENT: A time of decrease. Say your goodbyes. Clean. Let go.

Moon Rituals

The Full Moon is an especially potent time when shadows, secrets, and dreams are illuminated. It's an ideal time to charge your magical tools: tarot cards, rocks, your talisman bag, and amulets. Lay them outside or on a windowsill where they will be bathed in moonlight overnight. Say a prayer to the Moon:

Thank you for your mystery, for your silver light, for your gentleness and your beauty. Please guide my intuition.

You can also make Moonwater by putting a bowl of water outside to absorb the Moon's blessings. Add some herbs to the water if you'd like. In the morning, filter the water into a glass jar and secure the lid. Later, if you practice divination of any sort, you can prepare yourself by anointing the space between your eyes with a drop of your Moonwater. You could also use it for scrying (see page 173).

Following the Moon's cycles can heighten your magical connection to the powers beyond and within you. New Moons tend to be a good time to collect materials for your crafts, and Full Moons are ideal for creating, building, and manifesting.

If you speak it, you can make it happen!

CELEBRATIONS: PAST & PRESENT

At Midwinter, the nights are long, and families come together to remember and share the meaningful things in life. While Christmas and Hanukkah are two of the most widely celebrated Midwinter feasts, the Solstice can be observed no matter a person's faith or beliefs. In fact, it can be celebrated in addition to or instead of other religious holidays of the season!

SOL INVICTUS

Sol Invictus (meaning "unconquered Sun") originated in ancient Syria as a festival to celebrate the Sun god. Later, this holiday was adopted by Romans, who also worshiped the Sun as a life-giving god. It became a week-long festival called Saturnalia, during which time the Sun god was reborn. The shortest day of the year was cause for great celebration, as it meant the Sun god was returning, undefeated once again, and would now begin to regrow his strength.

YALDA

Yalda is a celebration of the sun's rebirth observed in modern-day Iran and beyond, but it dates back thousands of years. In ancient Iran, the longest night was thought to be an unlucky time when dark forces were at work. Traditionally, families would gather in their homes, remaining awake through the night to be sure nothing bad happened. Nowadays, it's still common to stay up late on Yalda, but the mood is less fearful and more focused on warmth and enjoyment. Families feast on reddish foods like pomegranates, persimmons, and dried fruit as their rosy color symbolizes the coming dawn. Many people recite poetry by the Persian poet Hafez on this night, sometimes using his books to practice a form of divination called BIBLIOMANCY. This involves opening the book to a random page, reading the poem there, and interpreting what messages it might hold for the reader.

Inti Raymi

Inti Raymi is a Winter Solstice festival celebrated by the Incan people of South America in June, the height of Winter in the Southern Hemisphere. Two GEOGLYPHS (stone lines) were carved into the ground, running more than a quarter-mile and framing the flat-topped adobe pyramid Cerro del Gentil as the Winter Sun set behind it. More than fifty other lines radiate from the center of Cerro del Gentil, some a mile long. It's like Cerro del Gentil is the Sun and the lines are its rays.

Inti Raymi celebrates the return of the Sun god Inti, though tribute is also paid to Pachamama, the Earth Mother. The holiday was both a celebration of the origin of the Incan people and the arrival of a new year. When the Spanish invaded Peru, they outlawed the holiday, but nowadays people have reclaimed it and recreated the traditions of their ancestors.

Junkanoo

Junkanoo, named after chief John Canoe who fought against European invaders in Ghana, is a carnival-like festival first observed by enslaved Africans in the Caribbean and the southern United States. While the plantation owners were busy celebrating Christmas and New Year's, enslaved people found ways to revive the traditions of their West African homelands.

In Ghana, one of the biggest holidays of the year was the New Yam festival, celebrating the December planting of this important crop. (Another yam festival was held in September when the yams were harvested.) Communal music was a crucial part of honoring and enjoying the occasion, so during Junkanoo, people remembered these traditions and gathered to play drums and dance.

Once slavery was abolished, Junkanoo celebrations became less common, but the holiday is still celebrated in the Bahamas.

SEASONS NEAR THE EQUATOR

The equator is an imaginary line that wraps around the middle of planet Earth. Because of Earth's tilt, the equator receives the same amount of sunlight throughout the year. For this reason, places near the equator don't experience Spring, Summer, Fall, and Winter like the rest of the globe. Instead, there is a wet season and a dry season. Some places experience significant daily downpours, so their wet season is called monsoon season.

Around the world, we experience different changes throughout a year, but all cultures develop unique stories and ways of life in relationship to their environment.

Other Planets

Do you wonder about other planets in our solar system and whether they have seasons, solstices, and equinoxes? Well, Venus's tilt is very slight, so there really isn't much variation as it spins around the Sun. Mars, on the other hand, has a similar tilt to our Earth's (about twenty-four degrees), but its orbit is more oval-shaped than round, so its seasons are more dramatic. Mercury's orbit around the Sun is very oval-shaped, kind of like an egg; so when it approaches the Sun, it gets super hot, but as it journeys farther away, it becomes extremely cold. The other planets in our solar system—Jupiter, Saturn, Uranus, and Neptune—are all so far from the Sun that they're cold all the time.

Mercury

Venus

Mars

SCAVENGER HUNT

PORTALS

In architecture, a portal is a doorway. How many stories have you read where a character discovers a secret portal and steps through it into a realm of magic and possibility? Think of the wardrobe leading to Narnia or Alice's rabbit hole to Wonderland.

A magical portal is a doorway to another world, other ways of being, or other ways of looking at things. You've been tapping into the magic of the world around you, connecting to it, and strengthening your own inner power by doing so. Don't be surprised if you start to see portals around you. You might see one in nature but not be able to enter; you might only get hints of what exists beyond it.

A patch of air that seems somehow strange and different,

Just as our magic is usually less flashy than what we encounter in books and movies, portals might also be more subtle. They can take the form of a puddle on the sidewalk reflecting the sky above, an archway made of tree branches, a hole in a bush, or a patch of air that seems somehow strange and different.

Think of your ability to notice them as a special power you've developed over time. Others may not be able to see what you see—and that's okay.

If you find a portal, don't just jump through it. Remember: whenever characters in books step through a portal, the stakes become higher and the ensuing journey entails more responsibility, risk, and danger.

You don't have to enter every door that opens to you. Instead, pause and consider if you're ready for whatever is on the other side. If you are, then close your eyes, take a breath, and take your first step forward!

a puddle on the sidewalk reflecting the sky, a hole in a bush.

PLANTS & ANIMALS OF THE SEASON

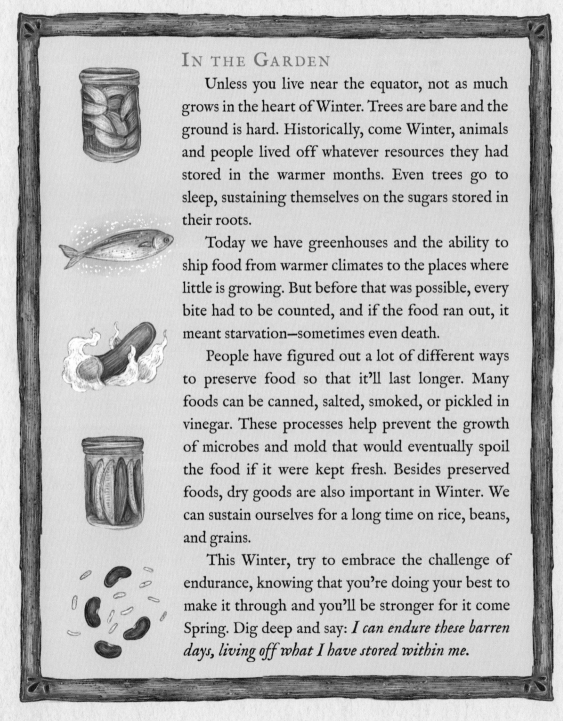

IN THE GARDEN

Unless you live near the equator, not as much grows in the heart of Winter. Trees are bare and the ground is hard. Historically, come Winter, animals and people lived off whatever resources they had stored in the warmer months. Even trees go to sleep, sustaining themselves on the sugars stored in their roots.

Today we have greenhouses and the ability to ship food from warmer climates to the places where little is growing. But before that was possible, every bite had to be counted, and if the food ran out, it meant starvation—sometimes even death.

People have figured out a lot of different ways to preserve food so that it'll last longer. Many foods can be canned, salted, smoked, or pickled in vinegar. These processes help prevent the growth of microbes and mold that would eventually spoil the food if it were kept fresh. Besides preserved foods, dry goods are also important in Winter. We can sustain ourselves for a long time on rice, beans, and grains.

This Winter, try to embrace the challenge of endurance, knowing that you're doing your best to make it through and you'll be stronger for it come Spring. Dig deep and say: *I can endure these barren days, living off what I have stored within me.*

FIRE CIDER

Makes: 1 *quart*

In the colder months, we tend to gather indoors, where germs can spread more easily. Fire cider is a folk recipe for building immunity—our bodies' natural defenses against illness. It's full of powerful nutrients that help our bodies fight harmful bacteria. No two batches of fire cider are exactly alike, so if you can't find some of the spices and herbs below, that's okay! Follow your intuition and think of it as an experiment.

You will need:

* 1 ginger root
* 1 horseradish root
* 1 turmeric root
* A variety of hot peppers, fresh or dried
* 1 lemon
* 5 or more garlic cloves
* 1 small onion
* 1 cinnamon stick
* 1 spoonful each of the following herbs and spices (dried or fresh): Oregano, thyme, cayenne pepper, rosemary, cloves, and rosehips
* Apple cider vinegar
* Honey

You will also need:

* A kitchen knife and cutting board
* A large glass jar with lid
* A sieve
* A drinking glass

1. Wash the roots, peppers, and lemon in the sink.

2. With an adult's help, use a kitchen knife and cutting board to carefully chop the roots and peppers into bits. Slice the lemon into discs. Mince the garlic and onion.

> Take Care: The seeds of some peppers contain an oil that can burn your skin, so wash your hands thoroughly with soap and water after handling them!

3. Add the roots, lemon, onion, garlic, cinnamon, herbs, and spices to a large glass jar. Top it off with apple cider vinegar and seal it with a lid.

4. Let your fire cider sit for at least a month in a dark cupboard or pantry. Give it a shake every day.

5. When the cider is finished brewing, filter out the plant material with a sieve.

6. Add a splash of fire cider and a teaspoon of honey to an 8-ounce glass of room-temperature drinking water. Stir and enjoy! Store your remaining cider back in the cupboard, where it will keep for about six months.

IN THE WILD
Microorganisms

Microorganisms are living things so small we can't see them, but they exist all over every surface on this planet, including your skin, and even inside your body! Certain species live in the coldest and hottest environments on Earth, where nothing else can survive. These are called EXTREMOPHILES because they love to live where no one else can!

5,000,000,000,000,00

Bacteria were some of the earliest forms of life on our planet, and with the help of microscopes, scientists have learned to recognize a great variety of color, shape, and size among these little creatures.

PSSt → There are about five quintillion bacteria on Earth—that's a five with thirty zeros after it, and yes, it's a real number!

Your body is like a planet for bacteria, hosting an entire ecosystem of different lifeforms. Scientists have determined that for every cell of your body, there's a microbial cell living alongside it—meaning "you" are as much bacteria as you are your own self!

Harmful bacteria enter your body through any openings they can find—sailing in on the air you breathe, catching a ride on the food you eat, or sneaking in through an open cut, for example. Once inside, the bacteria's goal is to take over and turn your body into a bacteria factory.

But your body doesn't want this to happen. Your little white blood cells identify the germs as dangerous intruders and gear up your immune system to fight. When you get a fever, your body is heating up to make itself inhospitable to bacteria.

Most bacteria aren't out to get you, though! In fact, many species of bacteria are your friends. For example, gut bacteria (the species that live inside your belly) help break down and digest food more easily. Fermented foods, like yogurt and pickles, are healthy because when you eat them, you're adding more friendly microbes to the party in your guts!

Outside the body, bacteria help break down material into soil. Sometimes, scientists even use bacteria to clean up pollution because they can eat toxins and turn them into substances that are safer for our planet. And since bacteria grows so quickly, it's also used to make some medicines.

Hint: The power of bacteria is a reminder that you don't have to see something for it to have real and significant effect!

WINTER SOLSTICE ALTAR

Suggested Items: Sprig of pine needles, yule log, pinecones, sticks of cinnamon, pomander ball, bells, holly

Colors to incorporate: Gold, red, white, green

During Midwinter, it's best to slow down and go through a period of quiet reflection. Be gentle with yourself and listen to your needs. With less sunlight, it can be a difficult time of year for many people.

Prayer is a way of sending good thoughts, hopes, and wishes to the people you love, including yourself. It's asking for help and protection from the bigger, invisible forces out there. You might have specific beings you pray to, or it may be more abstract. Maybe you don't believe in such beings at all. Regardless, keeping the people you care about in your thoughts is not only comforting—it has real benefits for all involved!

Imagine your loved one surrounded by a glowing light of protection. Visualize their face and body radiating with love and peace. If you ever have trouble falling asleep, you can practice this exercise in bed, cycling through the people you love, sending them your best wishes.

The same goodwill you send to those you love will glow and grow in your own heart.

MORE RITUALS FOR YULE

Make Your Own Ice Lantern

When the light of day is at its NADIR—its lowest point all year—people have traditionally encouraged the Sun's return by generating their own light from other sources: candles, bonfires, or in modern times, twinkle-lights! You can contribute to this symbolic celebration by making a lantern and shining it through the darkness.

Fire is thought of as a bridge between the Sky realm and the Earth realm, since it flickers and dances between the two. When you light a fire, you can think of yourself as communicating directly with the heavenly bodies—the Sun, Moon, planets, and stars. In this case, you're asking the Sun to return and shine its generous light upon the Earth.

Note: This activity involves lighting a fire. Be sure to
review the fire safety tips on page 76 before you proceed!

You will need:

❀ 1 large yogurt container
❀ 1 smaller yogurt container
that fits inside the larger one
(with at least an inch of space
between the two)
❀ Water

❀ Seasonal botanical objects:
small pinecones, pine needles,
decorative red berries,
holly, etc.
❀ 1 tea-light candle
❀ 1 stick lighter

1. Center the smaller yogurt container inside the big one. Fill the
space between the two vessels with water up to the edge of the
smaller container. Arrange the botanical pieces to your liking inside
the water.

2. If the weather is below freezing (32°F), set your lantern outside. If
not, place it in the freezer overnight.

3. The next evening, pry the smaller yogurt container out from the
bigger one. (You may need to place the whole thing in a bowl of warm
water to make it easier to pull them apart.) When you're finished, you
should have a circular block of ice that's hollow in the middle.

4. Find a special spot outside. Clear away any flammable debris like
dried leaves and sticks, and place your lantern on the ground. Set the
tea-light candle inside the lantern's hollow and, with an adult's help,
carefully light it with a stick lighter.

5. Slowly, your lantern will melt from the warmth of the light. As
it does, think of the energy and warmth of the candle's flame as
growing and returning to you.

Yule Log

To bring festive cheer (and some nice smells) into your home, it's great fun to decorate a Yule log. Traditionally, the Yule log is meant to be burned for warmth, and as a symbol of release and letting go. If you can do so safely with an adult, burning the Yule log is a meaningful ritual of reflection. The log, carefully decorated and imbued with love, is transformed into something new, providing warmth as it changes and disappears. Burning the Yule log reminds us that even though nothing is forever, things can continue to exist in new shapes and forms.

You will need:

* A log or a thick branch, preferably found on the ground in the park or woods
* Boughs of evergreen
* Pinecones
* Red and green yarn, gold and silver ribbon

Find a hefty branch that has fallen naturally and wrap it in the evergreen boughs, using the yarn and ribbon to secure them in place. You can also attach paper snowflakes and a pomander (page 206) to the log as you make them. Place the Yule log on your altar, or display it as a centerpiece on the table where you eat meals. You can surround it with holiday cards you make or receive as a reminder of the warmth of love.

PAPER SNOWFLAKES

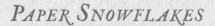

Paper snowflakes are a pleasing addition to a Yule log
and a festive Winter decoration. You can attach them
directly to your log, hang them in your home, or tape
them up in your windows to mimic falling snow.

You will need:
- ❁ 1 piece of paper (any color works, but white is often chosen to resemble real snowflakes)
- ❁ Scissors
- ❁ String or yarn (and/or tape)

1. Fold your piece of paper in half diagonally, making a triangle. Then fold it a couple more times, making smaller triangles.

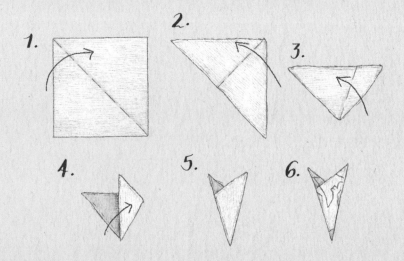

2. Without unfolding the paper, cut little shapes out of it: triangles, half-moons, squares, and circles. It's always a surprise when you unfold your paper and discover how your snowflake turned out! Repeat this process, making as many snowflakes as you wish.

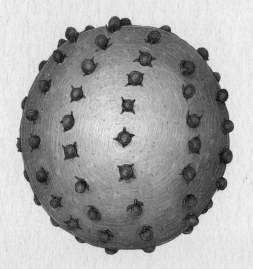

POMANDER BALL

Back in medieval times, POMANDERS (perfumed balls) were worn as necklaces or hung in the home to mask bad smells and ward off illness. While these aromatic ornaments can't really protect us from germs, the connection between the sweet, warm scent of the pomander and health and happiness abides. You can make your own pomander using an orange and cloves.

You will need:

* 1 orange
* A handful of whole cloves
* 1 long piece of ribbon
* Scissors

1. Poke the clove stems into the unpeeled orange so that the fruit is studded with the woody spice. You can pattern the cloves however you like: in lines that curve from top to bottom or in a spiral that wraps around the fruit, for example.

2. Insert a clove at the north pole of the orange. Tie your ribbon around that clove and attach the pomander to your Yule log or hang it elsewhere in your home—anywhere you'd like to infuse with a festive scent!

RITUAL BATH: YUZUYU CITRUS BATH

In Japan, the shortest day of the year is called toji. On this day, it's believed that as the light wanes, so does our good fortune. To counteract bad luck, people take baths called yuzuyu with herbs and yuzu—a citrus fruit that is ready to harvest right around the time of toji. The yuzu tree is strong and can survive freezing temperatures, so it's a symbol of endurance. In addition to protecting against bad luck, the yuzuyu bath is said to improve blood circulation, which in turn helps strengthen us against illness.

You will need:

❀ 3-6 yuzu fruits

> *Note:* These lumpy yellow fruits can often be found at an Asian market, but if you don't have one nearby, you can substitute oranges or grapefruit.

❀ A kitchen knife and cutting board

PSSSt It's best to take the yuzuyu bath in the evening before bed because it's so relaxing.

1. Using the kitchen knife and cutting board, carefully score the yuzu, oranges, or grapefruit. This means you want to scratch the surface of the peel so that the fruit will release some of its oils when it's added to the bath.

2. Fill the bathtub with warm water, being sure to follow the safety tips on page viii.

3. Drop the fruit into the tub, then lower yourself in.

4. Enjoy the clean, citrusy scent of the water as it softens your skin. Imagine the yellow fruits are tiny suns, infusing your bath with light and good luck!

IN JAPAN, BATHERS SAY
"ICHIYOU-RAIFUKU" (陽来復)
AS THEY SOAK, WHICH TRANSLATES
TO "RETURN OF SPRING" OR
"FAVORABLE TURN OF FORTUNE."

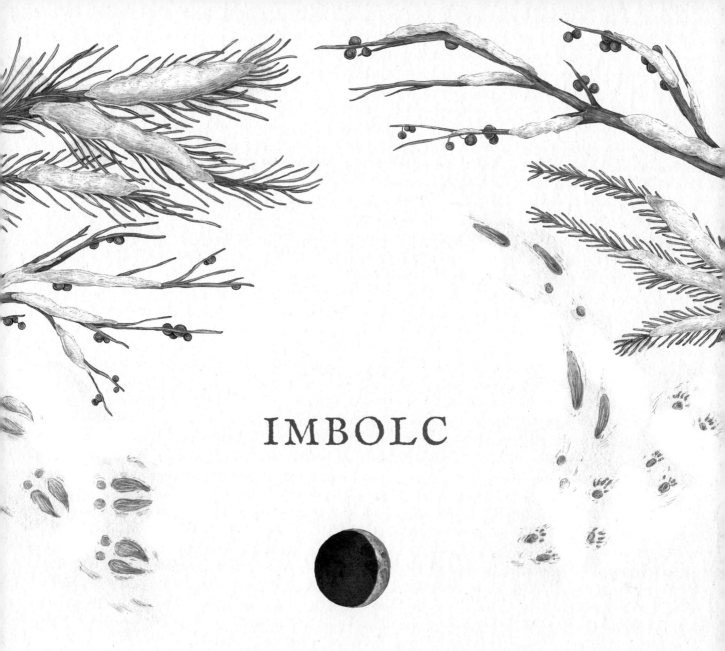

IMBOLC

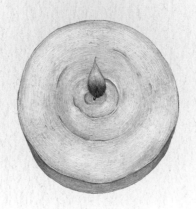

RHYTHM OF THE WHEEL

Come the first of February, it may feel like it's always been Winter and always *will* be Winter. But change is on its way! It doesn't seem like it, but the days *are* getting longer. Look closely: the signs of life are out there, beginning to stir, though they may be buried deep.

Imbolc is a cross-quarter fire festival, the midway point between the Winter Solstice and Spring Equinox. In ancient Ireland, it marked the first day of Spring. That might not make much sense if you live in a place where it's still cold and snowy at this time of year. But a transformation is underway. Slowly, the ground is softening. Soon, the birds will return. Sometimes we have to believe in things we can't see or prove but know in our hearts to be true. The Wheel is turning.

Imbolc gets its name from Old Irish words that mean "in the belly." It's also known as *Oimelc* (pronounced *Ee-mulk*), which means "ewe's milk." Either way, the holiday stands for growth in darkness and patience despite uncertainty. The air may be cold, but we know the Earth is warming, preparing to bear new life.

SPIRIT OF THE SEASON

Often, we're anxious to get through the darkest days, wishing for an end to the dreariness of Winter. But the Wheel of the Year is about accepting and finding the special in each season.

Good things take time. When we try to rush things, they'll often fall apart. Sometimes, it's better to sit with the situation, even if it's uncomfortable, to allow the truth to reveal itself to you in its own time.

Taking our time is not the same as doing nothing at all. It means listening deeply and allowing things to unfold naturally, as they're meant to. During Imbolc, the Earth is taking its time and inviting us to do the same. So relax, be patient, and trust that things will fall into place.

Remember:
Within every ending is a new beginning,
and in every beginning, we hold the
memory of what's come before.

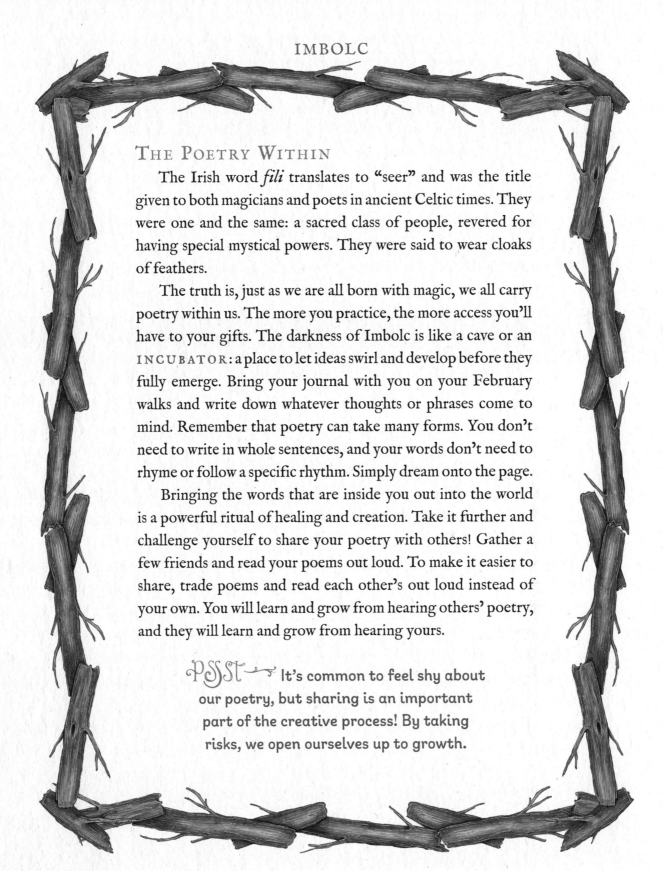

THE POETRY WITHIN

The Irish word *fili* translates to "seer" and was the title given to both magicians and poets in ancient Celtic times. They were one and the same: a sacred class of people, revered for having special mystical powers. They were said to wear cloaks of feathers.

The truth is, just as we are all born with magic, we all carry poetry within us. The more you practice, the more access you'll have to your gifts. The darkness of Imbolc is like a cave or an INCUBATOR: a place to let ideas swirl and develop before they fully emerge. Bring your journal with you on your February walks and write down whatever thoughts or phrases come to mind. Remember that poetry can take many forms. You don't need to write in whole sentences, and your words don't need to rhyme or follow a specific rhythm. Simply dream onto the page.

Bringing the words that are inside you out into the world is a powerful ritual of healing and creation. Take it further and challenge yourself to share your poetry with others! Gather a few friends and read your poems out loud. To make it easier to share, trade poems and read each other's out loud instead of your own. You will learn and grow from hearing others' poetry, and they will learn and grow from hearing yours.

PSSt ⁓ It's common to feel shy about our poetry, but sharing is an important part of the creative process! By taking risks, we open ourselves up to growth.

CELEBRATIONS: PAST & PRESENT

CANDELARIA

In Tenerife, an island off the west coast of Africa, Candelaria is a holiday celebrating the mother goddess. Long ago, two indigenous Guanche shepherds found a statue on a beach of a woman holding a baby in one arm and a green candle in the other. She was recognized as Chaxiraxi, the Guanche people's Sun mother goddess. The statue was installed in a cave and prayed to for protection against illness, droughts, and volcanic eruptions. Later, when Spanish colonizers invaded the island, Chaxiraxi became Mary, mother of Jesus, and the Guanche people blended the colonizers' Catholic beliefs with their own. Chaxiraxi-Mary kept her brown skin and is known as the Black Madonna and Our Lady of the Candle. Our Lady of the Candle is also the patron of the Philippines, another former Spanish colony, where she is celebrated on February 2.

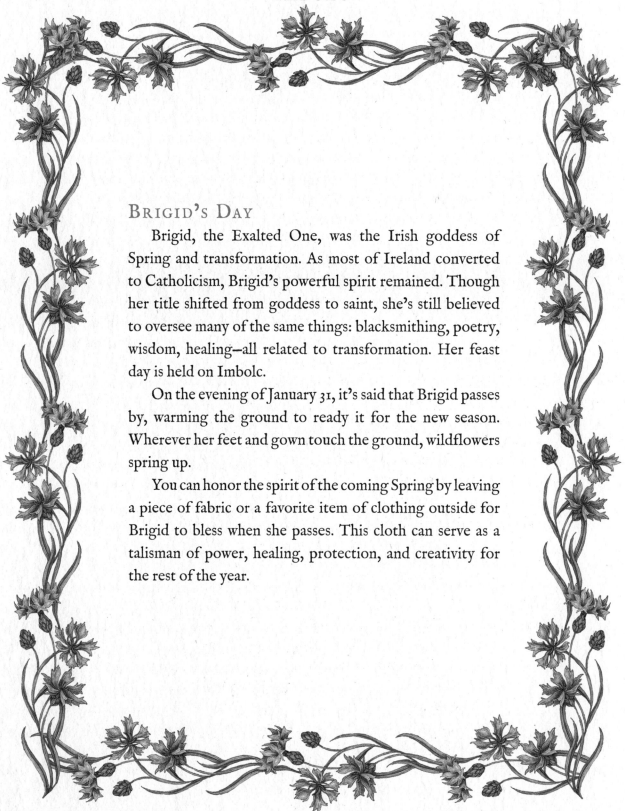

BRIGID'S DAY

Brigid, the Exalted One, was the Irish goddess of Spring and transformation. As most of Ireland converted to Catholicism, Brigid's powerful spirit remained. Though her title shifted from goddess to saint, she's still believed to oversee many of the same things: blacksmithing, poetry, wisdom, healing—all related to transformation. Her feast day is held on Imbolc.

On the evening of January 31, it's said that Brigid passes by, warming the ground to ready it for the new season. Wherever her feet and gown touch the ground, wildflowers spring up.

You can honor the spirit of the coming Spring by leaving a piece of fabric or a favorite item of clothing outside for Brigid to bless when she passes. This cloth can serve as a talisman of power, healing, protection, and creativity for the rest of the year.

Bridy Doll

Making an EFFIGY, or doll, of Brigid, goddess of Spring and transformation, is a powerful way to honor the incoming light. Allow her spirit of protection to help guide you through the changes of the season, reminding you of who you are at your core.

You can sew your Bridy doll out of cloth and stuff it with wool, cotton balls, or straw. If you have dried herbs from your Summer harvest you can add the leaves or flowers to the doll's insides. Not only will it make her smell nice, it's also a reminder of Summers past and the new one on its way.

Alternatively, you can make a Bridy doll out of paper, twigs, bark, leaves, and whatever other natural materials you find on your walks outside during this season. Many children like to make Bridy a bed, too, laying her down at nighttime and tucking her in safe and cozy.

CARNIVAL

In February or early March, many places observe Carnival: a vibrant celebration of celebration itself! People wear masks, make costumes, go on parade, and allow themselves to be as wild and free as their hearts desire. It's a time to live in the moment, make merry, and enjoy all life has to offer.

Originating with the Catholic religion, Carnival is celebrated all over the world. In New Orleans, Louisiana, people honor the holiday with weeks-long Mardi Gras parades, and in Brazil, samba groups perform dances for onlookers. Carnival takes place in the days leading up to Lent, a forty-day period of sacrifice, fasting, and ATONEMENT—asking forgiveness. In places that go through Winter, a time of natural deprivation, Carnival's bright colors and lively festivities stand out against the quiet grayness of the season.

LUNAR NEW YEAR

In China, which follows a lunar calendar, the second New Moon after the shortest day of the year announces the end of Winter and the coming of Spring. That's usually right around Imbolc, give or take a week or two. Houses are swept clean to make way for good fortune, families reunite for a big midnight dinner, and gifts are exchanged. The Chinese Lunar Year follows a ZODIAC cycle of twelve animals, starting with the rat, and ending in the dragon. Do you know what animal represents your birth year? Lunar New Year is celebrated in a variety of ways in other East Asian countries as well.

WEATHER PREDICTIONS

Because this season can vary so much from year to year, people have historically looked for signs to tell them what weather the coming days might bring.

In the United States, we rely on a groundhog named Punxsutawney Phil to tell us how much longer we have left of Winter. If Phil emerges from his burrow, sees his shadow, and returns to his hole, then we have six more weeks of Winter. If he doesn't, the milder weather of Spring is just around the corner.

In ancient Ireland, it was said that Cailleach the Crone, the hobbling witch goddess of Winter, went out to gather firewood on February 1. If the day was sunny and dry, she'd be able to gather a lot of wood. Winter would be prolonged because she'd take her haul back to her cottage, light a big fire, and continue to busy herself with her magic for the next six weeks. If the day was wet and gray, however, she wouldn't be able to gather much kindling, the wood damp and useless. She'd give up and make way for the goddess Brigid to usher in the warmer weather of Spring.

SCAVENGER HUNT

Imbolc is the threshold between Winter and Spring, a time when we're still in the heart of darkness but can start to make room for hope. The best way to celebrate Imbolc is to go for walks and look for subtle signs of change.

Notice the *GROUND*, how hard it is, and if this, too, changes day by day. Seek out melting.

Try to catch every sunrise or every sunset in a week.

The *SUN* might be hiding behind a veil of gray most days, its light hazy and dim, but it's there, biding its time and building its strength. Those two extra minutes every day add up!

Every day, new changes become visible. This time of year was called "the Quickening" in ancient Ireland, perhaps because in Winter everything seems so still and hidden; but once the world begins to stir, the changes gather momentum.

Look for hints of COLOR.
Are there any little nubs starting to form
on the tips of tree branches?

The breath of the sleepy planet is softening as it slowly prepares to AWAKEN.

Is the air beginning to smell a little different?

PLANTS & ANIMALS OF THE SEASON

TRACKING STORIES

To find out who's waking up and coming out of hibernation, look for animal tracks. As creatures start to emerge, you may not be able to see them out and about, but you can seek the traces of their movement.

If you live somewhere snowy, look for footprints in the snow. If there's no snow on the ground, observe sandy or muddy areas. Tracks tell a story if you know how to read them. Which direction are the tracks coming from? Where are they going? How fast was the animal moving?

This time of year, the story most tracks tell goes something like this: Someone is hungry so they braved the cold in search of food. Sometimes they aren't so lucky, and another hungry creature gets them first!

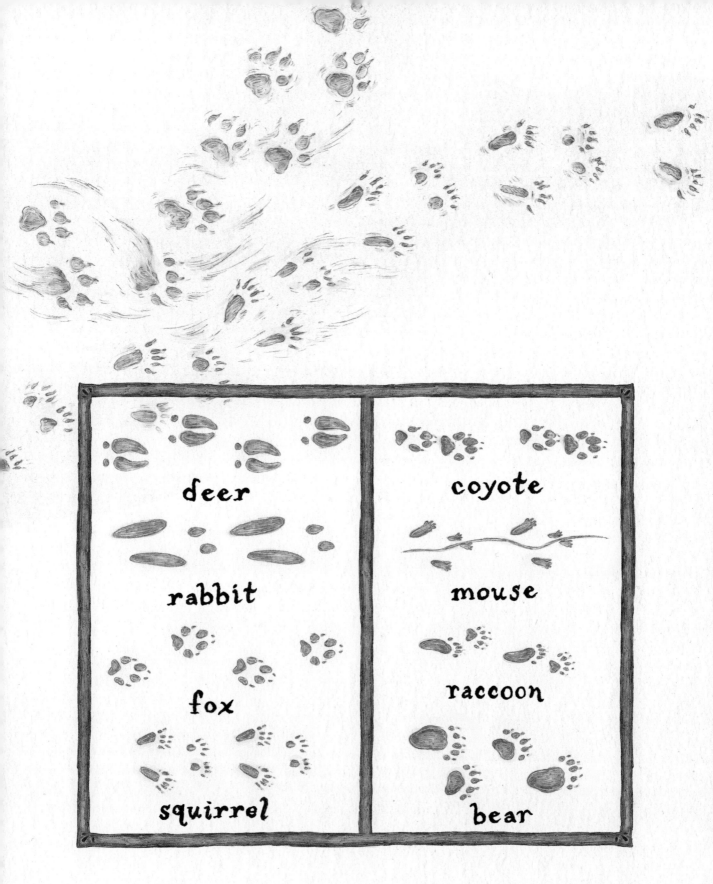

deer

rabbit

fox

squirrel

coyote

mouse

raccoon

bear

IN THE GARDEN

The greens and growth of Spring might feel a lifetime away, but it's never too early to start planning and dreaming about what you will plant!

It might not feel like you're doing much because planning exists in the invisible realm of thoughts and potential ... but without dreaming, nothing would get done. Preparation is an essential step to doing things properly.

Ask yourself these questions:

❖ *What do I want to plant, and where?*

❖ *What materials do I have?*

❖ *What do I need and where can I get it? What's my budget?*

❖ *Can I borrow or make things so I don't have to buy them?*

❖ *What went wrong last year, and how can I do it differently this year?*

Visualize your garden. Draw plans of it. Talk to people who might want to help you this year. Make a list of all the steps you will take. You can't predict everything, and you'll want to leave some things up to inspiration and chance, but thinking it through can help you make a strong start.

Peruse seed catalogs for new ideas. Just looking at the pictures of different plants and imagining your future garden will give you a warm and toasty feeling—as though Spring has arrived already!

Pssst It goes without saying:
Gardens are not the only things that benefit
from big dreams and thoughtful planning!

IN THE WILD

Befriending Trees

Trees grow slowly. They stand tall and witness the seasons change and return. They have many of the same needs as all living things: to breathe, to stretch, to grow, to feed and be fed. Trees are good listeners. They're not going anywhere with your secrets. They sway and tremble with feeling, but they're reliable. They've seen and experienced a lot. You can always count on a tree to stay right where it is, solid and living.

Find a tree that calls to you and get to know it. As you would with any friend, notice the details that make it special. Touch its bark. Talk to it. Listen to it. Come back every day for a week. Tell your tree something about yourself each time you visit. Wait for it to tell you something about itself in return. Read the tree one of your poems. Whisper to it something you've never told anyone else. Your secret is safe with the tree. It can hold your words in its trunk.

Maple Syrup

Real maple syrup is a gift from trees to our taste buds! Sap can only be collected during a short window of time when the days are above freezing, but the nights are still frigid. In many places, these conditions occur between Imbolc and Ostara. The rising temperatures create pressure in the tree's roots and trigger the sap to start flowing upwards. This happens in all trees in late Winter or early Spring, but the sap of the sugar maple is the sweetest.

Makers of maple syrup first drill upwards into the tree's trunk, about two inches deep, to where the sap flows.

PSSt This sounds like it might hurt the tree, but trees are very hardy. If done properly, it's not much different from a nurse drawing blood from your arm at the doctor's office.

A tap is inserted into the hole, and then a bucket is hung beneath the tap, so the sap drips right in.

Once the sap has been collected, it must be boiled down. The heat kills off any harmful bacteria, and as the water evaporates into steam, the sap condenses into syrup. It needs to boil for almost an entire day before it gets that sticky consistency we love. Forty gallons of sap make one gallon of syrup!

IMBOLC ALTAR

It's time to give your altar a thorough cleaning!

Clear the entire surface, but be gentle with every object. Make a batch of Moonwater (see page 190), and add a tablespoon of sea salt to the bowl. Soak any rocks, figurines, and coins from your altar in the bowl; scrub them with a soft cloth, then dry them with a clean towel. Wash the surface of your altar with a cloth, warm water, a splash of vinegar, and a drop or two of your favorite essential oil. Dust your photos, and replenish any water or plants. Lay down a clean altar cloth, and return the objects with care.

Suggested Items: Candles, your favorite poem handwritten on a scrap of paper, Bridy doll and bed, Brigid's cross, small bowl of milk, lantern

Colors to include: White, pale blue, pale pink, pale green

Standing before your altar, welcome the coming light. Take this time to enjoy a moment of quiet stillness. With permission, light a candle, and visualize its warmth filling your body and softening your heart. You've had to harden a bit to protect yourself through the darkness of Winter, but now you can allow your heart to open. It's time to thaw.

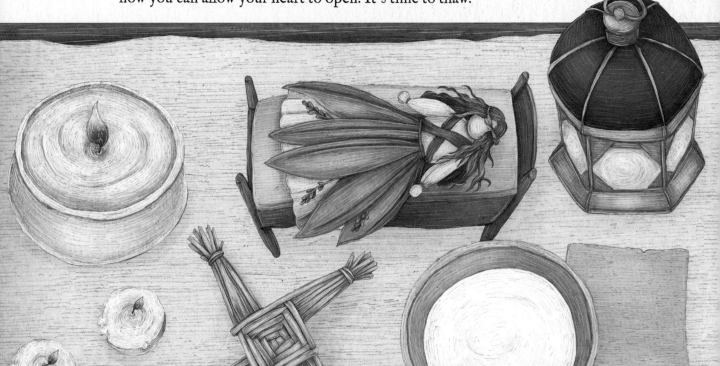

MORE RITUALS FOR IMBOLC

CANDLE MAGIC

Lighting candles is a powerful form of magic. Any time you work with candles in a magical way, there are many choices to consider: the color of the candle you burn, the words and images you draw on the glass or inscribe in the wax, the time of year, day of the week, and the phase of the Moon. Each of these elements can have meaning related to your goal.

First, decide what your goal is. You could think of your goal as a wish. What is it you'd like to manifest—to make real? Then, referring to the keys below, choose what color and timing best align with your wish.

Timing:

The English, Spanish, and French days of the week are named after Roman and Norse gods and goddesses. Consider these meanings when timing your candle magic.

◈ Monday/lunes/lundi: Day of the Moon

◈ Tuesday/martes/mardi: Day of Tyr (Norse god of justice) and of Mars (Roman god of war and victory)

IMBOLC

- Wednesday/miércoles/mercredi: Day of Woden/Odin (Norse god of wisdom) and of Mercury (Roman god of messages, communication, and travel)

- Thursday/jueves/jeudi: Day of Thor (Norse god of thunder) and of Jove/Jupiter (Roman king of the gods)

- Friday/viernes/vendredi: Day of Freya (Norse goddess of love and fertility) and of Venus (Roman goddess of love and beauty)

- Saturday/sabado/samedi: Day of Saturn (Roman god of wealth and discipline) and the day of sabbath, a time set aside for rest and worship

- Sunday/domingo/dimanche: Day of the Sun

Color:

- Red: power, victory, strength
- Pink: love, romance, sweetness
- Orange: joy, energy, creativity
- Yellow: happiness, abundance
- Green: growth, prosperity
- Blue: health, peace
- Purple: intuition, spiritual insight
- White: cleansing, purification
- Black: protection, warding off negativity
- Brown: grounding, stability

PSSST ⟿ **Before lighting any candles,
review the fire safety tips on page 76.**

Keep a close eye on how your candle burns:

- Is the flame strong, bright, and steady? That's a good sign that your goal is on its way to manifesting!

- If your flame is flickering and sputtering, your wish might need some more energy to come true. How might you help it along?

- If the flame blows out, the timing may not be quite right, or you may need to rethink your goal. Perhaps it's not meant to be at this time.

- Also watch how quickly the candle burns down. A fast-burning candle indicates a goal that's about to become a reality!

- When the candle is finished, examine the wax residue left in the bottom of the glass or candleholder. As you did in the tasseomancy exercise on page 162, see if you can decipher any symbols or messages.

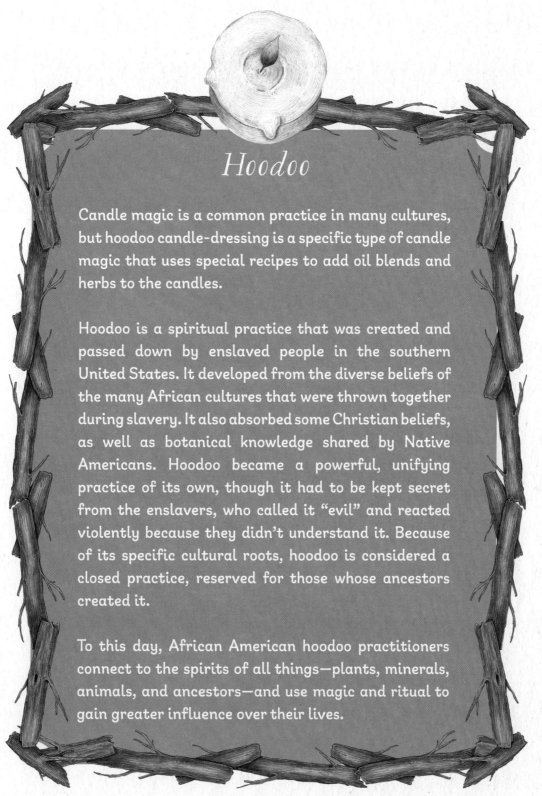

Hoodoo

Candle magic is a common practice in many cultures, but hoodoo candle-dressing is a specific type of candle magic that uses special recipes to add oil blends and herbs to the candles.

Hoodoo is a spiritual practice that was created and passed down by enslaved people in the southern United States. It developed from the diverse beliefs of the many African cultures that were thrown together during slavery. It also absorbed some Christian beliefs, as well as botanical knowledge shared by Native Americans. Hoodoo became a powerful, unifying practice of its own, though it had to be kept secret from the enslavers, who called it "evil" and reacted violently because they didn't understand it. Because of its specific cultural roots, hoodoo is considered a closed practice, reserved for those whose ancestors created it.

To this day, African American hoodoo practitioners connect to the spirits of all things—plants, minerals, animals, and ancestors—and use magic and ritual to gain greater influence over their lives.

Golden Pancakes

Makes: 6 to 10 pancakes

Imbolc is all about calling back the light. One delicious way to summon the warmth of spring is by whipping up your own batch of golden suns! Before you begin, let your family or friends know they're invited to a pancake feast in honor of the Sun's return. Set the table with a white tablecloth and candles.

To keep things simple, use a just-add-water pancake mix and follow the instructions on the back of the box, adding any extra ingredients you'd like (berries, nuts, sliced bananas, etc.).

You will need:
* Pancake mix
* Water
* Butter
* Maple syrup or honey
* *Optional:* 1 cup nuts, seeds, berries, bananas, chocolate chips . . . whatever you think will make your batch tastiest!

You will also need:
* A large mixing bowl
* A wooden spoon
* Frying pan
* Spatula
* Ladle

1. In a large mixing bowl, use a wooden spoon to blend the pancake mix and water according to the package instructions, then stir in any extra ingredients.

2. With an adult's help, melt a pat of butter in a pan over the stove.

3. Scoop out a ladleful of batter and gently pour it into the pan, forming a flat, round cake. Wait for the batter to start bubbling; that's how you know it's ready to flip! Use your spatula to flip the pancake. Let both sides get golden brown, then slide the cake onto a plate.

4. Repeat this process as many times as your batter will allow.

5. Serve your pancakes with butter and maple syrup or honey.

In France and elsewhere, Catholics celebrate Candlemas on February 2. Traditionally, the household's candles are blessed by the church on this day, marking the end of the Christmas season. Often, communities gather to share a feast of pancakes and crepes: round, gold, and warm like the returning sun!

MAKE YOUR OWN WITCH'S BROOM

Cleaning might sound like a boring chore, but it's an important element of magical practice. There's a reason witches are often pictured with BESOMS or magical brooms. Ahead of any magical or spiritual undertaking, it's important to SANCTIFY the space—make it holy and special. You may not know what spirits and energies surround and inhabit a location—you may not even believe in them or know if you do, and that's okay—but you can still honor a space by cleaning it. A good rule of thumb is to leave all places in better shape than you found them.

To make your broom, head out for a walk and gather fallen twigs and thin branches. Tall, dried prairie plants, such as evening primrose or blue vervain stalks, also work. Imagine you're the Cailleach, but instead of burning what you gather, you'll be making your stalks into a besom. While you're at it, be on the lookout for a longer, thicker branch to form your handle.

You will need:

* Several fallen twigs, thin branches, and/or dried prairie plants
* One longer, thicker branch
* A ball of twine
* Scissors
* *Optional:* Acrylic paints and paintbrushes, ribbons, and charms

1. Bundle the twigs around one end of the branch, holding them firmly with one hand. Use your other hand to wrap the twine around and around the bundle. After several turns, tie the twine in a knot and use your scissors to cut away the loose ends. Do this a couple of times so your besom is secure.

Note: If your bundle still feels a little loose,
try sticking a few more twigs into the besom
to make sure it's as tight as can be!

2. If you like, you can paint the handle of your broom and/
or decorate it with ribbons and charms to lend it some of
your personal magic.

3. Use your besom to sweep any area before you do magical
work. Take a moment to observe your space. Speak out
loud to it, thanking it for holding you. Start in the corners
of the room, casting out all stale and negative energy as
you sweep.

PSSST Slowing down and putting
your hands to work at a practical task can
help you to focus and be more present.
Your besom may not fly, but it can help
you feel freer and lighter in other ways!

Weaving with Reeds

Brigid's Crosses are another Imbolc tradition, woven from dried grasses
and hung above the front door to protect the home from hunger and
harm. They also represent the turning of the Wheel of the Year.

On your walks, keep a lookout for rushes—reeds, tall grasses, or weeds.
With a pair of gardening scissors, cut the stalks down near the base.

At home, clean the stalks of any leaves or dried flowers, so
that they're long, straight, and stick-like. Fill a shallow tray
with water, and soak the stems overnight to soften them.

1. Take a long, softened rush and hold it vertically in your left hand.

2. Take a second rush of similar length, and place it over the first horizontally.

3. Fold the second reed in half around the first, so that it wraps around the midway point of the first.

4. Turn the cross so that you're holding the folded rush vertically in your left hand.

5. Take a new rush, pinch it in half, and fold it around the vertical reed.

6. Turn the cross again, in the same direction, so the newest reed is now vertical and facing up.

7. Continue adding reeds in this way, until each arm has about five rushes, or until you're happy with the size of your cross.

Note: Tie the ends with string. If you'd like, trim the ends of the reeds to make a neater cross.

RITUL BATH: SOOTHING OAT MASK

After the long Winter, pamper yourself with a nourishing face mask. This will soothe and soften your skin, preparing it for the Sun's gentle kiss.

You will need:
- ¼ cup oatmeal
- Mortar and pestle
- A spoonful of milk
- A spoonful of honey
- Washcloth

1. Grind the oatmeal into powder using the mortar and pestle. Add milk little by little, until your mixture is the consistency of thin mud. Stir in the honey. Spread the mask over your face, avoiding your eye area.

2. After about 15 minutes, you'll wash the mask off with warm water. But first, while you're waiting for it to dry, lay down somewhere dark, resting a warm, damp washcloth over your eyes. Put on some peaceful music, and allow yourself to be still. Breathe. Relax your body.

You hold great power inside you. It's always with you; it's yours. Imagine it as light, growing inside your chest with every breath you take. It's as if you're stoking a fire in your heart.

YOU are MAGIC

You are strong, creative, and connected to all living things. You can shape your world for the better. Take care of yourself and all those you encounter.

ACKNOWLEDGMENTS

FROM FIONA:

One of the essential themes of the Wheel of the Year is that the whole is greater than the sum of its parts, especially when we share our gifts: nothing is done alone. Because of the support I had in writing this book, it grew from seed into a full, thriving garden.

Some specific thank-yous to the many heads and hands that helped this book blossom:

Thank you, Nicholas: a font of knowledge and insight, always there to help me shape, expand, and refine my ideas.

Thank you to my sister Caitlin and brother Andrew: early readers, constant inspirations.

To my kids, Icarus and Orpheus, and my niece and nephews, Saorla and Daithí, Evan and Elliana: thank you for being your wild, free selves; thank you for your sweetness and wonder! One of my hopes for this book is that it may offer different metaphors to help visualize and implement a healthier future for our beautiful planet and its inhabitants.

Thank you, Alyssa, my generous, dedicated, and incisive agent; Jessica, illustrative genius, whose exquisite talent brought my words to life; Melissa, sensitive and encouraging champion, whose belief made this book a reality. I am amazed by how lucky I've been to work with these women; it's been a shining example of the joys collaboration can bring. Thank you to all at Andrews McMeel who worked to make this happen. Thanks to Rebecca Tamás for planting the seed of connection in my mind between Ana Mendieta and the Green Man in her essay "On Greenness."

Thank you, also, to my dear friends Ruth, Stephany, Katrina, Guillermo, Malcolm, Nance, Sara, Carrie, Kara & Wojtek, Kate & Anthony, Rahnee & Mike. Much love and gratitude to each of you. Thanks to my parents for teaching us appreciation for nature and its rhythms in my own childhood.

Thanks to the public spaces: the parks, the gardens, the schools, the libraries.

Thanks, too, to the spirits that guide, support, protect, and surround.

FROM JESSICA:

I'm eternally grateful I was asked to work on this truly magical book. Illustrating Fiona's beautiful words has been one of my favorite projects to date, and I feel more in touch with nature and the world around me than ever before. Thank you, Fiona, for putting this into the world! Collaborating with you and our wonderful editor Melissa has been a true joy in my life; thank you both so very much. Thanks also to my agent Alyssa, for your continued support, encouragement, and generosity. A very big thank you to the incredible team at Andrews McMeel.

Thank you to my patient, kind, and generous husband Nick. Your support of my work and the long hours I put into every book means the world to me. Thank you for tending to the house, the garden, and our beloved Molly when I could not.

Thank you to Andi, my favorite witch, for your excitement, knowledge, and friendship. I'm so proud of you. Thank you to Kayla for your kind and thoughtful suggestions and help whenever I needed it. I would not be as good of an artist or as good of a friend without you.

Thank you to my family. Liana and Hannah, I am so grateful to you for listening to me and caring for me always. I am so lucky to have parents who are also my friends, who taught me to love and appreciate nature. You gave me the best advice I've ever been given: "Take a break and go for a walk." I love you all so much.

GLOSSARY

ACIDIC *(adjective):*
Having the qualities of an acid—a sour chemical substance (for example: lemon juice or vinegar)

AFFIRMATION *(noun):*
Words meant to encourage

ALCHEMY *(noun):*
The ancient, magical practice of transforming one substance into another

ALKALINE *(adjective):*
Having the qualities of an alkali—the opposite of an acid (for example: milk or baking soda)

ALLERGEN *(noun):*
Something that can cause an allergic reaction

ALTAR *(noun):*
A sacred place, often a table, decorated to encourage spiritual communion

ANCESTORS *(noun):*
Those who came before you

ARCHEOASTRONOMY *(noun):*
The study of how prehistoric cultures related to celestial patterns and built monuments to align with them

ARCHETYPE *(noun):*
A spirit or character that appears in many cultures, representing a deep truth of human experience

ATONEMENT *(noun):*
The effort to repair a wrong

AUSPICE *(noun):*
A spiritual sign

BESOM *(noun):*
A broom made of twigs

BIBLIOMANCY *(noun):*
a method of divination that uses books to receive messages

BIODIVERSITY *(noun):*
The variety among life on this planet

CARTOMANCY *(noun):*
A method of divining or interpreting information using cards

CELESTIAL *(adjective):*
Relating to the skies or universe, especially the planets and stars

CHLOROPHYLL *(noun):*
The green pigment found in plant leaves

COLLECTIVE CONSCIOUSNESS *(noun):*
The knowledge all beings share

COMPANION PLANTING *(noun):*
The practice of cultivating different plants together so they support one another's living conditions

COMPOST *(noun):*
Nutritious food for plants made of decomposed, once-living matter

COSMOS *(noun):*
The universe, including all stars and planets

CREPUSCULAR *(adjective):*
Occurring near dusk, as the sun is actively setting

DECOMPOSITION *(noun):*
The process of breaking down and turning into earth

DEFORESTATION *(noun):*
The widespread removal of trees

DIRECT SOW *(verb):*
To plant seeds into the ground instead of a planter or pot

DISPERSION *(noun):*
The act of spreading something across a wide area

DIVINATION *(noun):*
The practice of communicating with the universe, usually in order to receive guidance and insight

DRUIDS *(noun):*
Ancient Irish holy people who worshiped nature

ECOSYSTEM *(noun):*
All the living things that coexist within an area

EFFIGY *(noun):*
A doll

ELUSIVE *(adjective):*
Hard to catch, pin down, or fully understand

EMANCIPATION *(noun):*
Freedom from slavery

EPHEMERALITY *(noun):*
The idea that nothing is permanent, that everything changes

EXPLOITATION *(noun):*
The use of someone or something without adequate payment or respect

EXTINCTION *(noun):*
When every member of an animal species is gone forever

FAMINE *(noun):*
A lack of resources resulting in severe hunger

FERMENTED FOODS *(noun):*
Foods that use living microorganisms for preservation, health benefits, and/or taste (for example: yogurt and kimchi)

FEUDALISM *(noun):*
A system in which most people worked in harsh, exhausting conditions, while a few powerful people took more than their fair share of the harvest and profit.

FOSSIL FUEL *(noun):*
Natural fuel made from the ancient remains of living organisms (for example: coal, oil, and gas)

FUNGI *(noun):*
Mushrooms, yeast, and molds

GENIUS LOCI *(noun):*
The spirit of a place

GEOGLYPH *(noun):*
A mark of significance carved into rock or inscribed on the ground

GRIEF *(noun):*
The state of mind and being you experience after a significant loss

HIBERNATION *(noun):*
An extended period of deep rest

HIEROGLYPHIC *(noun):*
The picture-based written language of the ancient Egyptians

HOLISTIC *(adjective):*
Considering the body, mind, and spirit to be equally important and interconnected

HYDRA *(noun):*
A many-headed beast from Greek mythology that sprouts two new heads for every head that gets chopped off

IMMUNITY *(noun):*
a body's ability to defend against illness

HYPHA *(noun):*
A single string that together with others makes up mycelium

INCENSE *(noun):*
A natural material (such as resin or spice) that is burned as perfume or for spiritual cleansing purposes

INCUBATOR *(noun):*
An enclosed environment designed to protect and support new life

INDIGENOUS *(adjective):*
Native to a particular place

INTUITION *(noun):*
Inner knowledge that exists beyond conscious reason; the "gut feeling"

INVERSION *(noun):*
An upside-down position

KIN *(noun):*
People who share support and loving connection

NAIAD *(noun):*
Ancient Greek spirit of water

KINDLING *(noun):*
Small, dry material used to start a fire (for example: tiny twigs or crumpled newspaper)

LIMINAL *(adjective):*
Existing at a border or threshold, in a state of change or becoming

LUNAR *(adjective):*
Relating to the moon

MANIFEST *(verb):*
To make real, to bring into existence

MEDICINAL *(adjective):*
Having healing properties

MEDIUM *(noun):*
A person or material used to express or communicate an idea

MICROORGANISM *(noun):*
A living creature so small it cannot be seen without a microscope (for example: bacteria and viruses)

MUTUAL AID *(noun):*
When people help each other in an organized way

MUTUALISM *(noun):*
When beings help each other according to their needs and reserves

MYCELIUM *(noun):*
The weblike underground fungi network

NADIR *(noun):*
The lowest point

OBSERVATORY *(noun):*
A place for watching the stars and planets

OXYMEL *(noun):*
An herbal tincture made of equal parts honey and vinegar

PAPIER-MÂCHÉ *(noun):*
A sculpture material made from newspaper, flour, and water

PARASITE *(noun):*
Something that obtains resources by taking them from another organism

PAREIDOLIA *(noun):*
The tendency to see faces wherever you look

PERIPHERAL VISION *(noun):*
Our sight of what is beside us as we look straight ahead

PHOTOSYNTHESIS *(noun):*
The process by which plants turn sunlight into food

PILGRIMAGE *(noun):*
An intentional visit to a place of spiritual significance

POLLINATOR *(noun):*
Something that spreads a flower's pollen to another flower so that plants can reproduce (for example: bees, birds, wind)

POMANDER *(noun):*
A perfumed ornament

PREHISTORIC *(adjective):*
Occurring during the time before written language

PRIMAL *(adjective):*
Instinctive; possessing an ancient power

PROPHECY *(noun):*
Knowledge of something that hasn't yet happened

PROPHETIC *(adjective):*
Having the ability to predict the future or give information from the past

REAP *(verb):*
To gather or collect

REINCARNATION *(noun):*
The belief that after death the soul returns or continues in a different body or form

RENEWAL *(noun):*
Freshness; new energy

RESILIENT *(adjective):*
Being able to withstand or recover from challenges and hardship

REVERENCE *(noun):*
Spiritual respect

SANCTIFY *(verb):*
To make holy

SCAVENGE *(verb):*
To search for food or resources
among what's been discarded
or forgotten

SCYTHE *(noun):*
A tool for harvesting grain or grass

SEMIOTICS *(noun):*
The language of symbols

SHAMAN *(noun):*
A person who can communicate
among the nature world, spiritual
world, and human world

SMUDGING *(noun):*
The Native American term for a
smoke-cleansing ritual that uses
white sage

SOLIDARITY *(noun):*
The feeling that another's struggles
and triumphs are also your own

SUBCONSCIOUS *(noun):*
A deep part of the mind that
influences our feelings and actions
without our awareness

SYNCHRONICITY *(noun):*
An uncanny coincidence

TAROT *(noun):*
A specific form of cartomancy using a
set of 78 symbolic cards

TEND *(verb):*
To care for; to listen to; to pay
attention to the needs of something
or someone

THRESHOLD *(noun):*
The border-area between
two different things (places,
seasons, stages)

TINCTURE *(noun):*
A form of medicine made by soaking
plant matter in liquid for a period of
time, then straining it out

UNCANNY *(adjective):*
Not easily explained

UNCONSCIOUS *(adjective):*
Without waking awareness

WIDDERSHINS *(noun):*
The counter-clockwise direction
(the opposite direction of the sun's
movement)

ZENITH *(noun):*
The highest point

ZODIAC *(noun):*
A calendar based on symbols that
are said to classify and influence
the seasons